Thinkquiry Toolkit 1

Second Edition

Thinkquiry Toolkit 1

Reading and Vocabulary Strategies for College and Career Readiness

Second Edition

A Wiley Brand

Published by Jossey-Bass

A Wiley Brand

One Montgomery Street, Suite 1000, San Francisco, CA 94104-4594—www.josseybass.com

Jossey-Bass books and products are available through most bookstores. To contact Jossey-Bass directly call our Customer Care Department within the U.S. at 800-956-7739, outside the U.S. at 317-572-3986, or fax 317-572-4002.

Wiley publishes in a variety of print and electronic formats and by print-on-demand. Some material included with standard print versions of this book may not be included in e-books or in print-on-demand. If this book refers to media such as a CD or DVD that is not included in the version you purchased, you may download this material at http://booksupport.wiley.com. For more information about Wiley products, visit www.wiley.com.

ISBN: 978-1-119-12751-2

9781119127789 PDF

9781119127772 ePub

Printed in the United States of America

SECOND EDITION

PB Printing   10 9 8 7 6 5 4 3 2 1

CONTENTS

About PCG Education   xi

Acknowledgments   xiii

Introduction   1

PART 1: Overview of the Common Core State Standards for English Language Arts and Literacy and the Related Instructional Shifts   6

Introduction to the CCSS ELA & Literacy   6

Instructional Shifts Required by the CCSS ELA & Literacy   8

Key Elements in the Standards and Shifts   11

PART 2: Selecting the Right Tools for Maximum Learning   17

Content Teachers Are Key to Supporting Students to Become Better Readers, Writers, and Thinkers   17

Why *Thinkquiry* Tools Work with Students in Grades 4–12   18

The Literacy Demands of Different Content Areas   23

The Connection between Vocabulary Development and Reading Comprehension   25

Tips for Using *Thinkquiry* Tools in Your Classroom   28

Designing Lesson Plans That Increase Content Learning   34

Evaluating Classroom Practice   38

Notes   43

Part 3: Laying the Foundation *before* Reading/Learning   44

Introduction   44

Knowledge Rating Guide   46

Knowledge Rating Guide Template   48

Knowledge Rating Guide Content Examples   49

Frayer Model   55

Frayer Model Example   56

Frayer Model Template   57

Frayer Model Content Examples   58

Triple-Entry Vocabulary Journal   59

Triple-Entry Vocabulary Journal Template   61

Triple-Entry Vocabulary Journal Content Examples   62

Word Sort   69

Word Sort Template   71

Word Sort Content Examples   72

Word Analysis   74

Word Analysis Template   76

Word Analysis—Frequent Affixes and Roots   77

Common Greek and Latin Roots in English   78

KWL Plus   80

KWL Plus Template   82

KWL Plus Content Examples   83

Quick Write   86

Quick Write Content Examples   88

Partner/Small Group Vocabulary Preview   89

Partner/Small Group Vocabulary Preview Template   91

Interactive Word Wall   93

Interactive Word Wall Planning Template 95

Interactive Word Wall Content Examples 97

Chapter Preview/Tour 101

Chapter Preview/Tour Template 102

Chapter Preview Content Examples 104

Anticipation/Reaction Guide 105

Anticipation/Reaction Guide Template 107

Anticipation/Reaction Guide Content Examples 108

Use of *Triple-Entry Vocabulary Journal* in a High School Science Classroom 109

PART 4: Building New Knowledge *during* Reading/Learning 112

Introduction 112

Question-Answer Relationship (QAR) 114

Question-Answer Relationship (QAR) Content Examples 116

Coding/Comprehension Monitoring 124

Coding/Comprehension Monitoring Template 126

Coding Content Examples 127

Two-Column Note Taking 133

Two-Column Note-Taking Template 135

Two-Column Note-Taking Content Examples 136

Question the Author (QtA) 143

Question the Author (QtA) Template 145

Question the Author (QtA) Content Examples 146

Analytic Graphic Organizers 147

Analytic Graphic Organizers for Vocabulary Development 150

Analytic Graphic Organizers for Patterns and Relationships   151

Analytic Graphic Organizers Content Examples   152

Semantic Feature Analysis   160

Semantic Feature Analysis Template   162

Semantic Feature Analysis Content Examples   163

Discussion Web (Social Studies)   164

Discussion Web Template   166

Discussion Web Content Examples   167

Proposition/Support Outline (Science)   168

Proposition/Support Outline Template   170

Proposition/Support Outline Content Examples   171

Inference Notes Wheel (English Language Arts)   172

Inference Notes Wheel Template   174

Inference Notes Wheel Content Examples   176

Think-Pair-Share   177

Think-Pair-Share Template   178

Think-Pair-Share Content Examples   179

Reciprocal Teaching   181

Reciprocal Teaching Template   183

Reciprocal Teaching Content Examples   184

Paired Reading   185

Paired Reading Content Examples   187

Critical Thinking Cue Questions   188

Critical Thinking Cue Questions Content Examples   193

Use of *Coding/Comprehension Monitoring* in an Elementary Social Studies Classroom   194

PART 5: Expanding and Deepening Understanding *after* Reading/Learning   **197**

Introduction	197
Role-Audience-Format-Topic (RAFT)	199
Role-Audience-Format-Topic (RAFT) Template	201
Role-Audience-Format-Topic (RAFT) Content Examples	202
Sum It Up	204
Sum It Up Template	206
Sum It Up Content Examples	207
Picture This!	210
Picture This! Template	212
Picture This! Content Examples	213
Save the Last Word for Me	214
Save the Last Word for Me Template	216
Save the Last Word for Me Content Examples	217
Give One, Get One, Move On	219
Give One, Get One, Move On Template	221
Give One, Get One, Move On Content Examples	222
Jigsaw	225
Jigsaw Template	227
Jigsaw Content Examples	228
Group Summarizing	229
Group Summarizing Template	231
Group Summarizing Content Examples	233
Problematic Situation	234
Problematic Situation Content Examples	236

Use of *Sum It Up* in an Elementary Mathematics Classroom   238

Use of *Save the Last Word for Me* in a Middle School English Classroom   240

References   243

Additional Resources   246

ABOUT PCG EDUCATION

A division of Public Consulting Group (PCG), PCG Education provides instructional and management services and technologies to schools, school districts, and state education agencies across the United States and internationally. We apply more than 30 years of management consulting expertise and extensive real-world experience as teachers and leaders to strengthen clients' instructional practice and organizational leadership, enabling student success.

As educators engage with rigorous standards for college and career readiness, PCG Education partners with practitioners at all stages of implementation. We work with clients to build programs, practices, and processes that align with the standards. Our team of experts develops and delivers standards-based instructional resources, professional development, and technical assistance that meet the needs of all learners.

In response to a wide range of needs, PCG Education's solutions leverage one or more areas of expertise, including College and Career Readiness, multi-tier system of supports/response to intervention (MTSS/RTI), Special Programs and Diverse Learners, School and District Improvement, and Strategic Planning. PCG's technologies expedite this work by giving educators the means to gather, manage, and analyze data, including student performance information, and by facilitating blended learning approaches to professional development.

To learn more about PCG Education, visit us at www.publicconsultinggroup.com.

$$PCG \mid \textit{Education}$$

ACKNOWLEDGMENTS

The resources and materials in *Thinkquiry Toolkit 1* were developed and field-tested by Public Consulting Group's staff and consultants. Special thanks to Katanna Conley, Christine Anderson-Morehouse, Doris Bonneau, Brianne Cloutier, Betty Jordan, BJ Kemper, Mary Ann Liberati, Jennie Marshall, Kevin Perks, Melvina Phillips, Kimberly Schroeter, Pamela Thompson, Roz Welzer, Susan Ziemba, Sharon DeCarlo, Rebecca Stanko, Peter Seidman, and Elizabeth Maine.

Key support for this work was provided by Nora Kelley, Barbara Hoppe, Elizabeth O'Toole, Diane Stump, and Caitlin D'Amico.

Julie Meltzer, Dennis Jackson, editors

INTRODUCTION

Welcome to the Common Core edition of *Thinkquiry Toolkit 1*. First published in 2010, *Thinkquiry Toolkit 1* is a collection of teacher instructional practices, student learning strategies, and collaborative routines that improve reading comprehension and vocabulary learning in grades 4–12. To be selected as a *Thinkquiry Toolkit* tool, the practice, strategy, or routine had to be research based, high impact, multipurpose, and effective in improving student learning across multiple content areas.

These tools are tried and true. Our consultants and classroom teachers have been using them for the past 20 years in multiple settings including high schools, career and technical education centers, middle schools, elementary schools, rural schools, urban schools, suburban schools, and digital academies. These tools support the reading comprehension and vocabulary development of all students.

A lot has happened in the past 6 years. In 2009, at the same time the first edition of *Thinkquiry Toolkit 1* was nearing publication, a sweeping initiative was under way that would change the face of English language arts and literacy instruction across the United States—the development of the Common Core State Standards. Launched in 2009 by state leaders, including governors and state commissioners of education from across the country, the development of the standards was intended to ensure that "all students, regardless of where they live, are graduating high school prepared for college, career, and life" (Common Core State Standards Initiative, 2015a). The Common Core State Standards in English Language Arts and Literacy in History/Social Studies, Science, and Technical Subjects (CCSS ELA & Literacy) were released in June 2010 and over the course of the next 2 years were adopted and implemented by the majority of states and territories.

In this newest edition of *Thinkquiry Toolkit 1*, we explain the implications of the CCSS ELA & Literacy for ELA and content literacy instruction, and we affirm the strategies and approaches in *Thinkquiry Toolkit 1* that can help implement the needed shifts in literacy instruction. As ELA teachers and teachers of literacy in other disciplines begin to align their instruction with the CCSS ELA & Literacy, they will continue to need tools, approaches, and strategies to support their students—and they will continue to use *Thinkquiry Toolkit 1* for those resources. In this edition of *Thinkquiry Toolkit 1*, we have added a new section that provides an overview of the CCSS ELA & Literacy and related instructional shifts, and we have explained how the research-based, experience-tested strategies and approaches in *Thinkquiry Toolkit 1* continue to provide a strong resource for helping students and teachers achieve the literacy requirements of the Common Core.

What Has Changed, and What Remains the Same in *Thinkquiry Toolkit 1*?

In 1999, we were asked what the next most important issue was going to be in education—that is, what needed to be addressed to ensure that students had the opportunities to be successful in college, in the workplace, and as citizens. Our answer: content area literacy.

We did not mean "basic reading skills"—although these are certainly necessary. We meant the ability to read, write, speak, listen, and think well enough to learn whatever one wanted to learn, demonstrate that learning, and transfer that learning to new situations.

Clearly, there were literacy skills that applied across all content areas and literacy demands specific to each content area. The Common Core affirms this vision. The standards recognize that literacy does not reside solely in the ELA classroom. In order for students to be ready for college and career when they graduate high school, they need to be proficient in the literacy skills of each discipline. The CCSS were not written just for ELA but for literacy in the disciplines as well.

In order to write *Thinkquiry Toolkit 1,* we compiled strategies and approaches that taught students how to read, write, discuss, and think in each content area. Teachers across the country began using these tools with their students in grades 4–12 and gave us feedback as to what worked well, how they used the tools, and the challenges they faced while teaching the strategies. We developed the materials in *Thinkquiry Toolkit 1* to provide directions, templates, examples, and scenarios based on teacher requests.

The purpose of the teacher instructional practices and collaborative routines included in this book is to help students develop the skills they need to be excellent readers, learners, and thinkers. The goal of teaching the learning strategies is for students to be able to use the strategies appropriately and independently when reading and learning new content. Similarly, in the Common Core, independence with grade-level text and skills is the ultimate goal.

We believe that *Thinkquiry Toolkit 1* will be an increasingly valuable tool for individual teachers, teams, departments, and whole schools. This edition of *Thinkquiry Toolkit 1* includes nearly all of the strategies, routines, and tools from the original. However, we have updated some of the examples to be more illustrative of Common Core practices, and we have added "Common Core Connections" to the strategies to help link the instructional shifts and key elements of the standards. The biggest change in this edition is the addition of a substantive Common Core section as Part 1 of this book. The intent of Part 1, Overview of the Common Core State Standards for English Language Arts and Literacy and the Related Instructional Shifts, is to frame teachers' use of *Thinkquiry Toolkit 1* as a Common Core resource. If teachers collaboratively take on these instructional practices, student learning strategies, and routines, teach them to students, and use them regularly across content areas, students will develop confidence and competence as readers, writers, and learners.

Format of the Toolkit

Thinkquiry Toolkit 1 includes five parts: Overview of the Common Core State Standards for English Language Arts and Literacy and the Related Instructional Shifts, Selecting the Right Tools for Maximum Learning, Laying the Foundation *before* Reading/Learning, Building New Knowledge *during* Reading/Learning, and Expanding and Deepening Understanding *after* Reading/Learning. Part 1 provides a description of the instructional shifts and key elements of the CCSS ELA & Literacy and makes connections between the shifts and *Thinkquiry* strategies. Parts 2–4 each correspond to one of three phases of reading instruction—before, during, and after—and provide tools that students and teachers can use to develop the habits and skills needed in that phase. The following is a brief overview of the contents of each part of *Thinkquiry Toolkit 1*.[1]

Part 1: Overview of the Common Core State Standards for English Language Arts and Literacy and the Related Instructional Shifts

In Part 1, we provide an introduction to the origin, purpose, and structure of the CCSS ELA & Literacy and an explanation of the instructional shifts teachers are required to make in order to fully implement the standards. We provide detail about each shift, the rationale for the shift, and how it relates to the standards. We also provide a more thorough explanation for several key elements shared by the instructional shifts: text complexity, academic language and vocabulary, and close reading.

Part 2: Selecting the Right Tools for Maximum Learning

In Part 2, we provide information that is key to using the *Thinkquiry* tools effectively. The tools are powerful but they have to be carefully selected and explicitly taught for students to use them to their greatest advantage. Part 2 includes topics such as:

- Why content teachers are key to literacy learning
- Why strategies matter
- The literacy engagement instruction cycle
- The literacy demands of different content areas
- The connection between vocabulary development and reading comprehension
- The research about vocabulary learning and reading comprehension
- The *gradual release of responsibility model*

---

[1] Content about how to support students before, during, and after reading/learning is adapted from the Council of Chief State School Officers (2010) *Adolescent Literacy Toolkit*. Available from http://programs.ccsso.org/projects/adolescent_literacy_toolkit/.

- Matching the right tool to the type of text students are reading
- Differentiation—what to do when there are students at different reading levels in the same class
- Designing lesson plans that support vocabulary development, improve reading comprehension, and increase content learning

Part 3: Laying the Foundation *before* Reading/Learning

The tools in Part 3 focus on preparing students for reading and learning by

- Considering what students already know about a topic
- Setting a purpose and generating questions for learning
- Attending to text features, graphs and charts, appendices, and other text structures that contribute to the student's understanding
- Adjusting understanding about text as new information is presented

Part 4: Building New Knowledge *during* Reading/Learning

The tools in Part 4 help students comprehend content information and construct concepts and relationships by

- Questioning to clarify and deepen understanding
- Monitoring understanding and using fix-up strategies, such as rereading, reading on, or examining a word more closely
- Making connections with other texts and integrating knowledge of world issues to make sense of text
- Inferring to get a deeper understanding of text and making valuable connections with the text
- Drawing conclusions and refining them in light of additional information
- Analyzing story structure and informational text structures and using these structures as supports for building meaning

Part 5: Expanding and Deepening Understanding *after* Reading/Learning

The tools in Part 5 help learners reflect on, analyze, and synthesize the content by

- Reflecting on what they read
- Reviewing information, ideas, relationships, and applications to real life by rereading, summarizing, and discussing with others
- Synthesizing by combining ideas and information within and across texts
- Presenting concepts learned through the informal and formal written and spoken word, including small-group classroom venues and authentic audiences

Each section's tools are listed in the section introduction. Note that many of the *Thinkquiry* tools can be used to support student learning at more than one phase of the reading process. How and when you and your students use the tools will depend on your teaching and learning goals, the needs of your students, and the specific demands of the text or content being read or learned.

The Tools of the Toolkit

Parts 3–5 of the Toolkit describe three types of tools: student learning strategies, collaborative routines, and teacher instructional practices.

Student learning strategies are strategies that we want students to be able to use independently in school and beyond. These strategies have the capacity to improve students' literacy habits and skills with ongoing use. For example, when students go to college and career, we want them to be able to use **Coding/Comprehension Monitoring**, **Two-Column Note Taking**, or **Sum It Up** strategies if these would be helpful to the task.

Collaborative routines support the social nature of literacy and learning by providing protocols for pair and group work. These help students use one another as a resource for learning. Collaborative routines shift the responsibility for learning to students and help students to improve their reading comprehension and vocabulary development when regularly engaged as part of teaching and learning.

Teacher instructional practices are approaches that teachers can use to support all students to develop the reading, vocabulary learning, and thinking skills of strong readers, writers, and thinkers.

Each tool is described with steps for implementation and tips for how to deepen student learning or maximize effectiveness. Templates are provided where applicable. For each tool, there is a set of examples of what the tool might look like "in action" in grades 4–12 in various content areas. Finally, at the end of each section, there are more extended classroom scenarios.

Professional learning and use of *Thinkquiry Toolkit 1* can take many different forms:

- *Individual teachers* of students in grades 4–12 can use *Thinkquiry Toolkit 1* to improve their students' reading, writing, vocabulary development, and content learning.

- *Professional learning communities, grade-level teams, teaching teams, or departments* can use the Toolkit by discussing student literacy needs and selecting strategies, collaborative routines, or instructional practices that address specific learning goals. Then teachers can try the approach in their classrooms. When they meet, they can discuss how they used the strategy, routine, or practice, how students responded, and how they would improve their instructional use of the tool next time. Teams can examine student work resulting from use of the tool to understand the impact of the tool on learning, related to the targeted standards.

- *School literacy leadership teams, departments, grade-level teams, or teaching teams* can select a common set of *Thinkquiry* strategies to teach students, thereby developing a set of common experiences and language for talking about literacy and learning. Students would see the applicability of the tools across content areas and strengthen their literacy habits and skills.

We hope that teachers find *Thinkquiry Toolkit 1* to be helpful in supporting their efforts to improve students' academic language and vocabulary, reading comprehension, and learning across the content areas.

PART 1: Overview of the Common Core State Standards for English Language Arts and Literacy and the Related Instructional Shifts

The Common Core State Standards for English Language Arts and Literacy in History/Social Studies, Science, and Technical Subjects (CCSS ELA & Literacy or "the standards") have been widely adopted or adapted in the majority of states across the country. This research-based set of standards raises the bar for what students will learn in each grade and sets the expectation that all students can and will achieve college and career readiness. As schools and districts begin to align curriculum and instruction with the CCSS ELA & Literacy, they review and reconsider the instructional activities, tools, protocols, and materials they currently use. In this same spirit, we revisited the tools, strategies, and instructional approaches in *Thinkquiry Toolkit 1* to confirm its alignment with the rigor of the CCSS ELA & Literacy and its accompanying instructional shifts. This trusted collection of high-quality, research-affirmed strategies, tools, and approaches continues to be a valuable resource for teaching and learning in the Common Core era both for current users of *Thinkquiry Toolkit 1* and for those who are seeing it for the first time. This new section of *Thinkquiry Toolkit 1* describes the instructional shifts required by the CCSS and connects them to the *Thinkquiry* strategies, tools, and approaches.

In this section, we provide an overview of the instructional shifts as well as what they mean for teachers, students, and instruction. Understanding the instructional shifts will help you most effectively choose the right *Thinkquiry* tools.

Introduction to the CCSS ELA & Literacy

The CCSS ELA & Literacy is a clear set of college and career-ready standards for kindergarten through twelfth grade. Published in 2010, the standards were developed under the auspices of state education chiefs and governors in 48 states; teachers, parents, school administrators, and experts from across the country provided input into the development of the standards. The standards are based on research and evidence and are built on the strengths of previous state standards. They are "based on rigorous content and the application of knowledge through higher-order thinking skills" (Common Core State

Standard Initiative, 2015c). The intent of this new set of high standards was to provide consistent, clear expectations across the states and to ensure that all students would have the knowledge and skills necessary to succeed in college and career.

Thirty-two College and Career Readiness anchor standards (CCRA) form the basis for all of the standards. They are organized in four domains: Reading (10), Writing (10), Speaking & Listening (6), and Language (6). Grades K–5 also include a set of standards for Reading Foundational Skills. At each grade level (elementary) and grade band (secondary), a detailed set of standards is built backward from these anchor standards. Reading standards are further divided into Reading for Literature and Reading for Informational Text. Additionally, the Reading standards (informational only) and Writing standards are made more specific for history/social studies, science, and technical subjects.

Each domain of the standards contains clusters of standards with a similar focus.

Reading

Key Ideas and Details, Craft and Structure, Integration of Knowledge and Ideas, and Range of Reading and Level of Text Complexity

Writing

Text Types and Purposes, Production and Distribution of Writing, Research to Build and Present Knowledge, and Range of Writing

Speaking & Listening

Comprehension and Collaboration, and Presentation of Knowledge and Ideas

Language

Conventions of Standard English, Knowledge of Language, and Vocabulary Acquisition and Use

Not only is each grade-level standard built on the one in the grade before it, the standards within and across domains relate to and integrate with one another. For example, the Language standard L.3 explicitly states, "Students will use their knowledge of language and its conventions when writing, speaking, reading, or listening." This integration appears throughout all of the standards, emphasizing the reciprocal relationships among the domains.

The standards clearly demonstrate what students are expected to learn at each grade level, but they do not dictate how to teach the skills and content. These rigorous standards represent a challenge not only for students but for teachers as well. Teachers need support to help students achieve this new, high set of standards and be able to read, discuss, and write about increasingly complex texts. *Thinkquiry's* strategies, routines, and practices are tools teachers will use to scaffold students toward independence and success in the standards.

Instructional Shifts Required by the CCSS ELA & Literacy

The CCSS ELA & Literacy require shifts in curriculum and instruction from teaching to earlier standards. These changes comprise three instructional shifts:

1. Regular practice with complex text and its academic language

2. Reading, writing, and speaking grounded in evidence from text, both literary and informational

3. Building knowledge through content-rich nonfiction

These shifts are closely related, contain overlapping elements, and have sometimes been stated as six, eight, or even ten "shifts." The three previous statements are the most common ways in which the shifts are characterized; they serve as a useful foundation for discussing the changes teachers and students must make in order to achieve college and career readiness in literacy.

Instructional Shift 1: Regular Practice with Complex Text and Its Academic Language

The CCSS ELA & Literacy set an expectation that students will be able to read and comprehend increasingly complex texts as they progress through the grades. **Text complexity** refers to the comprehension challenge of a text; complexity is measured both quantitatively and qualitatively. The more challenging and sophisticated a text is, the greater its complexity. The CCSS create a staircase of increasing text complexity so that students are expected to both develop their skills and apply them to more and more complex texts (Common Core State Standards Initiative, 2015b). Previous standards increased the level of literacy tasks from grade to grade but did not weigh in on text complexity at each grade. As a result, students often ended their high school grades reading texts that were below the level of complexity they were expected to read in college and career. The authors of the CCSS ELA & Literacy sought to remedy this gap by setting grade-level expectations for text complexity.

One of the factors that most influences text complexity is the text's academic language and vocabulary. In order to comprehend more complex texts students must be able to understand the vocabulary in the text and negotiate the overall structure of the text, its paragraphs, and its sentences. Of particular concern is **academic vocabulary**—sophisticated words that relate to specific disciplines and words that appear in multiple contexts but may not be familiar in everyday speech. Students whose vocabulary is limited will also be limited in understanding increasingly complex texts. Therefore, the standards are clear in their expectations that teachers will guide students in learning high-utility vocabulary, including knowing how to define words by using clues in the context in which they appear. This emphasis on vocabulary, while always implicit in ELA & Literacy standards, has been made explicit in the CCSS ELA & Literacy.

The need to increase text complexity at K–12, and the close relationship between text complexity and academic language, explains why Instructional Shift 1, Regular Practice with Complex Text and Its

Academic Language, is so important. *Thinkquiry* strategies, practices, and routines help students acquire and use academic vocabulary as well as organize, navigate, and comprehend complex text.

A more detailed discussion of text complexity and academic vocabulary appears later in this section.

Instructional Shift 2: Reading, Writing, and Speaking Grounded in Evidence from Text, Both Literary and Informational

The CCSS ELA & Literacy focus strongly on the role of evidence-based responses. Previous standards did not emphasize the use of textual evidence, and teachers often encouraged students to draw from their own experiences or feelings rather than from the texts. However, beginning in the earliest grades, the Reading, Writing, and Speaking & Listening standards set an expectation that students will collect evidence from texts and deploy it skillfully to support their writing and discussions. This emphasis prepares students for the demands of college and career, where much of the writing and presentation requires students to take a position or inform others while citing evidence, rather than personal opinion.

This shift has become associated with the practice of **close reading**: "Close analytic reading stresses engaging with a text of sufficient complexity directly and examining meaning thoroughly and methodically, encouraging students to read and reread deliberately" (Partnership for Assessment of Readiness for College and Careers, 2015). Aligning instruction with the CCSS requires teachers to create carefully sequenced series of text-dependent questions and tasks, scaffolding students toward deeper understanding of texts. Students further deepen their knowledge and understanding through structured, evidence-based discussions. As a result, students spend more time reading and learning from text and, in doing so, their ability to read and learn from text increases.

Related to this shift is a change in the focus of writing as well. Whereas many writing curricula emphasize narrative writing, the CCSS ELA & Literacy place a strong emphasis on argument and explanation, both of which require textual evidence to be effective. In writing, this shift places an increased focus on the informative and argument genres, using textual evidence to inform written claims. Finally, the speaking portion of this shift focuses on rich student discussions that are grounded in text-based understandings.

Instructional Shift 2 asks teachers to consider carefully how they ask students to think about and respond to text. This requires them to take notes, summarize, and organize information from the text. It requires students to build the skills and stamina for reading closely, rereading, and determining the explicit and inferred meanings in text. Students learn to annotate text, examining both the details and the big picture, and make connections based on their reading of a text through writing and discussion.

Instructional Shift 2, Reading, Writing, and Speaking Grounded in Evidence from Text, Both Literary and Informational, is one of the most challenging, yet most crucial, changes in teaching and learning from earlier sets of standards. *Thinkquiry* strategies, practices, and routines help students locate and organize evidence to use in writing and discussion.

A more detailed discussion of close reading appears later in this section.

Instructional Shift 3: Building Knowledge through Content-Rich Nonfiction

The CCSS ELA & Literacy have placed an increased focus on the deliberate use of content-rich nonfiction. This change in focus recognizes both the emphasis on nonfiction reading in college and career as well as the role of nonfiction in building student content knowledge. When students read increasingly complex texts with similar content, they build disciplinary knowledge and vocabulary.

Before the advent of the CCSS, reading in elementary schools was regularly taught as a subject separate and unrelated to content areas often through fictional text—stories, poetry, and chapter books. In other core subjects, such as science and social studies, students were more likely to learn content through direct instruction or by reading a textbook. At the secondary level, the teaching of reading was associated primarily with English class. Teachers of other disciplines often felt that they were experts in content but less well prepared to teach reading. Thus, reading was taught mainly in English and primarily through the genre of fiction. As a result, students were likely to be passive recipients of content knowledge, rather than learning how to build knowledge for themselves through text.

The CCSS ELA & Literacy, recognizing the prevalence of fictional text in elementary schools and the reliance on ELA teachers for reading instruction in secondary schools, call for a change in the balance of fiction and nonfiction in elementary schools and for shared responsibility for reading instruction across the secondary disciplines.

In grades 6–12, ELA standards place much greater attention on literary nonfiction in addition to literature. Additionally, in grades 6–12, specific standards for literacy in history/social studies, science, and technical subjects ensure that teachers of these disciplines share responsibility for reading instruction. The ultimate goal is that students will independently build knowledge in each discipline through reading and writing.

In grades K–5, meeting the standards requires a balance between literary and informational reading, primarily content-rich nonfiction in history/social studies, science, and the arts. The K–5 standards strongly recommend that students build general knowledge by reading texts on the same or similar topics, within each year and across years.

Reading and comprehending informational texts is generally more difficult for students than reading literature. Rather than a familiar story structure, informational text provides the challenges of complex text structures and dense content. To build knowledge independently from text, students will require scaffolds in the form of teacher modeling, tools, and repeated experiences with the text through a *gradual release of responsibility model*.

Instructional Shift 3, Building Knowledge through Content-Rich Nonfiction, is an important shift in raising students' content knowledge and reading ability. Allowing students to grapple with new content and complex structures in informational text is far more effective than frontloading knowledge through teacher lecture or other forms of disconnected notes or information. *Thinkquiry* strategies, practices, and routines support teachers and students in increasing disciplinary vocabulary and knowledge in a domain through content-rich nonfiction.

Key Elements in the Standards and Shifts

Several key elements appear within and across the CCSS ELA & Literacy and related instructional shifts. These elements differentiate the CCSS ELA & Literacy from previous standards and necessitate changes in practice as well. In this section of Part 1, we will explain more thoroughly three elements that are most critical to understanding and effectively teaching the standards: **text complexity**, **academic language**, specifically academic vocabulary, and **close reading**. Although these elements were introduced in relation to specific instructional shifts in earlier sections, they are not exclusive to those shifts; rather, the attention to text complexity and vocabulary appears throughout the standards. Similarly, **close reading** is a necessary change in practice implied by the standards and related to all of the instructional shifts. The "Key Element" sections will make clear the connection between these elements, the shifts, the standards, and the *Thinkquiry* tools.

Key Element: Text Complexity

CCRA.R.10: *Read and comprehend complex literary and informational texts independently and proficiently.*

This standard represents one of the most significant changes from earlier standards and raises the level of rigor for all students. Previous ELA and literacy standards did not mention text complexity, nor was the expectation that text complexity would increase throughout the grades ever explicitly stated. In the CCSS, the level of text students will read in each grade is explicit and the complexity of text increases from grade band to grade band.

The primary goal of the CCSS is to prepare every student for college and/or the workplace upon their graduation from twelfth grade. In 2006, ACT reported that on its college admissions test, the clearest differentiator of students who met or exceeded benchmark scores from those who did not was their ability to answer questions associated with complex text. This report supports a body of research related to the importance of text complexity. The Appendix of the CCSS ELA & Literacy details extensive research indicating that while the level of text complexity has risen at the college and career levels over the past 50 years, the overall complexity of texts at the K–12 level has decreased in difficulty. Additionally, students at the college level read complex text independently, while high school students are often heavily supported in doing so. In order to address the complexity gap between high school and college texts and students' ability to read and comprehend independently, the standards set high expectations for both complexity and independence in standard R.10 (Common Core State Standards, 2010).

Defining Complexity

The standards define text complexity with a three-part model that includes quantitative and qualitative factors as well as considering the characteristics of the reader and the task that is being required of the reader.

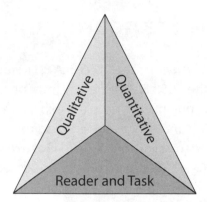

Figure 1.1: The Standards' Model of Text Complexity

Quantitative Factors

Of the three factors, quantitative measures are easiest to ascertain. These include such aspects of text complexity as word length, sentence length, and word frequency. Quantitative complexity is best measured with computer software. While there are many tools available to measure quantitative complexity, each uses somewhat different factors and algorithms for a particular type of text. Therefore, quantitative complexity is not a fixed number. One common tool is the Lexile measure (MetaMetrics, 2015). With the advent of the CCSS, Lexile ranges for each grade level or grade band have been adjusted upward so that the end point for the 11–12 grade band now aligns with the expectations at the college and career readiness level. This increase in expectations, resulting in a broader Lexile range for each grade, is often referred to as a "stretch" Lexile band. Because quantitative measures are concrete, they are the most common way to report complexity. Although tools to measure complexity have become more sophisticated and can measure variables beyond simple length and frequency of words and sentences, they still cannot fully ascertain the overall complexity of text. To do so also requires some human judgment.

Qualitative measures of text complexity require decision making by a human reader. There are four qualitative factors to be taken into account. Each factor is considered on a continuum of difficulty from easy to difficult, and most texts measure high or low in some different factors.

Qualitative Factors

Levels of meaning (literary texts) or purpose (informational texts). A literary or informational text with a single layer of meaning will be easier to understand than one with multiple layers of meaning. In literary texts, such dual layers of meaning may occur, for example, in a work of satire in which there is a literal message on the surface with a different underlying message. Informational texts, while appearing factual on the surface, are often influenced by political, philosophical, or historic points of view that provide an underlying message.

Structure. The structure of a text is the way in which it is organized. Texts of low complexity tend to have simple, conventional structures, while texts of high complexity have hidden, or unconventional, structures. For literary text, complexity increases with the use of devices, such as flashbacks, that deviate from chronological sequence. In informational text, structures that are more complex are often discipline specific and may contain complex graphics whose interpretation is essential to understanding the text.

Language conventionality and clarity. Texts that use straightforward, contemporary, everyday language are easier to understand than texts that use challenging language; for example, language that is archaic, figurative, domain specific, or misleading.

Knowledge demands. Texts that are easier tend to explain or provide whatever background knowledge is necessary to understand the texts. Texts that make many assumptions about the readers' prior knowledge or understanding are more qualitatively complex.

Reader and Task Considerations

Of all of the text complexity factors, this is the most dependent on the individual judgment of the teacher. A text may be easier or harder depending on the student who will be reading it, the purpose for reading, and the task that will be accomplished as the result of reading. A student who is knowledgeable in the content of a text or structure of a particular genre will find it easier to comprehend than would a student whose experience in that subject is more limited. Motivation, and a student's willingness to persevere in reading about a subject that does *or does not* interest him or her, can also affect the perceived difficulty of a text.

Text Complexity and *Thinkquiry*

Many of the strategies, practices, and routines in *Thinkquiry Toolkit 1* help students approach and comprehend complex text. Teacher practices, such as **Critical Thinking Cue Questions** (see Part 4) or **Chapter Previews** (see Part 3), provide models and scaffolds for approaching complex text. Student learning strategies, such as **Question-Answer Relationship (QAR)** (see Part 4) and **Coding/ Comprehension Monitoring** (see Part 4), help students analyze and organize complex text. In addition, collaborative routines, such as **Jigsaw** (see Part 5), provide peer support and motivation for working with complex text.

Key Element: Academic Language and Academic Vocabulary

Instructional Shift 1 refers to "complex text and its academic language." With the implementation of the CCSS ELA & Literacy, the term *academic vocabulary* is also used, sometimes interchangeably with *academic language*. While the terms are related, and both are important to the standards, these two terms differ. Academic language is the language used in textbooks, in classrooms, in sophisticated texts, and on assessments. It is different from everyday speech. Academic language includes a variety of formal-language skills and structures—such as vocabulary, grammar, punctuation, syntax, discipline-specific terminology, or rhetorical conventions—that allow students to acquire knowledge and academic skills. The standards place a high importance on academic language, explicitly within the Language standards, CCRA 1–3, and implicitly in the Reading, Writing, and Speaking & Listening standards. The Reading standards in the "Craft and Structure" cluster—CCRA 4–6—draw attention to words and phrases as they are used in a text, the structure of texts, and how point of view or purpose shapes a text; these standards all ask students to dig deeply into the academic language of the text.

Academic vocabulary is a subset of academic language and refers to the actual words and phrases, rather than to the structure of written language. It is widely recognized that a poor command of academic vocabulary is a main barrier to student comprehension of complex texts. The CCSS set very clear expectations for teachers to teach vocabulary and students to learn. Language standards L.4 and L.5 are specific at each grade level with regard to determining the meaning of unknown words, multiple-meaning words, figurative language, word relationships, and nuances in word meaning through a variety of means, including word analysis, context clues, and the use of reference materials. Additionally, L.6 says that students should "acquire and use accurately a range of general academic and domain-specific words."

Standard L.6 further differentiates vocabulary into "academic and domain-specific" words. Briefly, domain-specific vocabulary is the technical vocabulary of a particular discipline or field of study. Domain-specific words and terms are relatively low-frequency content words that appear mainly in texts addressing that particular domain. Words such as *brontosaurus, dynasty, isobar, feudalism,* and *polyhedron* are considered domain specific. General academic vocabulary comprises high-utility words that appear across multiple disciplines and are vital to carrying meaning. Although general academic vocabulary crosses disciplinary lines, it may not be used the same way in different contexts. For example, *rational* is used differently in a math text, a psychology text, and a work of fiction. General academic vocabulary also includes words that are more likely to appear in text than speech and give more specificity to common terms. For example, color words like *ecru* and *scarlet* may not be in a student's everyday speech. General academic vocabulary also includes process verbs, like *analyze* or *summarize,* and nouns, such as *capacity* and *assumption.* Students need access to the meanings of these more sophisticated words that do not appear frequently in their casual conversations.

The Appendix of the CCSS ELA & Literacy uses a well-respected framework to help sort out general academic from domain-specific vocabulary. Beck, McKeown, and Kucan (2002) divide words into three tiers:

Tier 1 includes words that are part of everyday speech for most native speakers of English.

Tier 2 includes more sophisticated high-frequency words that appear across multiple content areas (for example, *analyze, justify, fortunate, industrious, evidence, commit*).

Tier 3 includes low-frequency, discipline-specific vocabulary. Words and phrases that generally appear in relation to a particular content area (for example, *denominator, fossil, ballot, magma*) are considered Tier 3 words. We learn Tier 3 words as we learn a particular topic within a content area.

While both Tier 2 and Tier 3 words carry meaning and are vital to comprehension, the CCSS emphasize instruction in Tier 2 vocabulary because it is often neglected in favor of Tier 3 vocabulary, which is easier to identify.

Some of the many research-based tools included in *Thinkquiry Toolkit 1* that support deep learning of academic vocabulary as well as discipline-specific vocabulary are **Word Analysis**, **Interactive Word Wall**, **Frayer Model**, **Word Sort**, and **Knowledge Rating Guide** (see Part 3 for these tools).

Key Element: Close Reading

We have looked at three shifts—the "text complexity/vocabulary shift," the "evidence" shift, and the "nonfiction" shift. Yet whenever there is a discussion of Common Core–aligned instruction, **close reading** is usually mentioned. The term *close reading* is often coupled with the term *text-dependent questions*.

What is close reading?

The Partnership for Assessment of Readiness for College and Careers ([PARCC], 2012) defines *close reading* as engaging with a text of sufficient complexity directly and examining meaning thoroughly and methodically. In order to read closely, students must read and reread deliberately. Focusing student attention on the text itself empowers students to understand the central ideas and key supporting details. It also enables students to reflect on the meanings of individual words and sentences; the order in which sentences unfold; and the development of ideas over the course of the text, which leads students to arrive at an understanding of the text as a whole. Additionally, PARCC states, "A significant body of research links the close reading of complex text—whether the student is a struggling reader or advanced—to significant gains in reading proficiency and finds close reading to be a key component of college and career readiness."

Why do the CCSS ELA & Literacy make the expectation for close reading explicit?

In recent decades, pedagogy often emphasized the importance of teaching general metacognitive strategies in reading (for example, "What do good readers do?"). Metacognition is important, and good readers must seamlessly employ strategies that help them think about what they are doing when reading. However, as often happens with a good thing, in some classrooms the strategies became an end in themselves. Particularly concerning was an overemphasis on making connections in lieu of deeply understanding the text. Although good readers do make text-to-text, text-to-world, and text-to-self connections, they do so as they read and to deepen understanding, not as a stand-alone activity. When "making connections" is prioritized, students are not really probing into the deeper meaning of the text; they are treating the text more as a launch pad for their own thoughts than a text worthy of exploring in itself.

While teaching under previous curriculum frameworks with less explicit requirements, teachers sometimes defaulted to "making connections" in order to make the reading task easier for students and to keep them engaged by bringing the discussion to a personal level. Additionally, teachers were concerned that when asked to provide evidence-based answers, students would not be able to read well enough to produce those answers. It was more affirming to ask personal-response questions, or allow students to approximate an evidence-based answer, based on what they thought the book said. The CCSS recognize that in order to learn to read independently and comprehend deeply, students must develop the habits and skills of close reading.

How can teachers help students learn to read closely?

Close reading takes time, which can be in short supply in a classroom, and perseverance, which needs to be nurtured and supported. In order to teach students to read closely, teachers must know the texts well and must allow time in the text. They require students to read, and reread, each time with a purpose, and they provide structures for doing so. Close reading requires teachers to provide support as a scaffold to move students toward independence, rather than as a crutch to prop them up. The intent of a scaffold is that it will be removed when the structure can stand on its own. By carefully structuring text-dependent tasks and questions, teachers can lead students into deep understanding of a text as well as guide them toward being able to read closely on their own. Teaching and modeling how to read closely provides a scaffold that enables students to be able to read complex text independently. Examples of *Thinkquiry* student learning strategies that particularly support close reading are **Question-Answer Relationship (QAR)**, **Two-Column Note Taking**, and a variety of **Analytic Graphic Organizers** that help students make meaning of complex text. Collaborative structures such as **Reciprocal Teaching** and **Paired Reading** allow peers to help one another make meaning in close reading (see Part 4 for these tools).

If close reading is so important to the Common Core, why isn't it one of the instructional shifts?

The answer is that close reading is an instructional practice that is necessary for achieving all of the standards, and it is implied by the standards and the instructional shifts. CCRA.R.1 states that students will "Read closely to determine what the text says explicitly and to make logical inferences from it: cite specific textual evidence when writing or speaking to support conclusions drawn from the text." This standard sets the bar and creates an umbrella for the remaining reading standards, laying out the expectation that students will dig deeply, reread, and persevere in finding layers of meaning within parts of a text and the text as a whole. CCRA.R.1 also provides the foundation for deploying evidence in writing and discussion and for pursuing the meaning of words and phrases in the Language standards. With CCRA.R.1, CCRA.R.10 bookends the Reading standards: "Read and comprehend complex literary and informational texts independently and proficiently." In order to get from R.1 to R.10, students must learn to read independently and complete increasingly complex tasks with increasingly complex texts. In order to build these capacities, teachers help students learn to read closely by creating and posing deliberate sets of text-dependent questions and tasks. The practice of close reading is a bedrock for the standards and instructional shifts.

The Common Core State Standards for English Language Arts and Literacy reflect the skills and knowledge students will need to succeed in college, career, and life. Knowing how the standards differ from previous standards—and what the instructional shifts entail—will help in planning Common Core–aligned units and lessons. Understanding the purpose of the shifts will also support teachers in selecting *Thinkquiry Toolkit 1* strategies and practices to achieve student learning goals. Each tool in *Thinkquiry Toolkit 1* can be used in multiple ways for multiple purposes. In Parts 3–5 of the Toolkit, we have added a "Common Core Connection" to introduce each strategy; these are anecdotal notes for how the strategies and practices can support particular instructional shifts and key elements.

PART 2: Selecting the Right Tools for Maximum Learning

What is the best time to use Analytic Graphic Organizers?

Why does the Toolkit focus on vocabulary and reading comprehension at the same time?

What can I do when I have some students who read just fine and others in the same class who cannot read the text?

I am a content teacher—how can I help students' improve their reading comprehension?

Teachers across the country have asked these and many other questions related to content reading and learning. Before we get to the sections of the Toolkit that describe and provide examples of the actual tools, it is important to address many of the issues that concern math, science, social studies, and English language arts teachers—as well as their colleagues who teach foreign language, technical arts, fine arts, business, health, music, and other subject areas. It is easy to expect that all content area teachers focus on improving reading comprehension and vocabulary development. It is harder to provide practical guidelines for how teachers might do that in ways that increase student engagement and content learning. In this section of the Toolkit, we try to do that. We begin with a discussion of why content area teachers need to use the *Thinkquiry* tools.

Content Teachers Are Key to Supporting Students to Become Better Readers, Writers, and Thinkers

Why do all teachers need to support the ongoing literacy development of their students?

> The purpose of *Thinkquiry Toolkit 1* is to provide teachers with the tools to support students to become stronger readers, writers, and thinkers about the content they need to learn.

It is important that teachers in all disciplines understand their roles in strengthening students as readers, writers, and learners. There are four critical reasons why teachers need to become more effective at developing students' literacy abilities as an integral part of teaching and learning in each content area—and why, collectively, content area teachers need to provide the significant support to students for ongoing content literacy development (Irvin, Meltzer, & Dukes, 2007):

1. Teachers in each discipline know their content.

2. Teachers know the reading, writing, speaking, and thinking demands of the content they teach.

3. Teachers have the access and the opportunity—they see students regularly.

4. Teachers and their colleagues have the collective power to make a real difference in the amount of content reading and writing students do—and the amount and quality of supportive instruction they receive.

The purpose of *Thinkquiry Toolkit 1* is to provide teachers with the tools—the teacher practices, student learning strategies, and collaborative routines—that will support students to become stronger readers, writers, and thinkers about the content they need to learn.

Why *Thinkquiry* Tools Work with Students in Grades 4–12

> When you combine *Thinkquiry* tools with interesting reading and writing assignments, authentic reasons to read and write, and opportunities to engage in meaningful inquiry about a topic, students become engaged in the learning.

The Role of Motivation and Engagement in Literacy and Learning

Many studies suggest that students in the middle and upper grades, particularly boys, read less than they did when they were younger. When asked why, students indicate reasons including lack of interest in the assigned reading, lack of confidence in their own abilities as readers, and difficulty understanding the text (whether print or electronic, literary or nonfiction; whether the information is presented primarily through words or visuals). *Thinkquiry* tools are designed to help students increase their confidence in reading text, their proficiency in reading, and their engagement with the text. When teachers combine the tools with interesting reading and writing assignments, authentic reasons to read and write, and opportunities to engage in meaningful inquiry about a topic, student engagement typically soars.

It is also true that students will have difficulty comprehending reading materials if they lack the vocabulary necessary to read it. If a student does not understand "the language," it is much harder to have any deep understanding of the text. When the brain is not able to make sense of a situation, it disengages, making it hard to learn from text. Building background knowledge along with teaching and practicing academic, technical, and conceptual vocabulary helps build students' confidence that the assigned reading and learning is, in fact, doable. Thus, the *Thinkquiry* tools that assist with vocabulary development can have a positive effect on students' engagement with the text.

Reading about a topic independently and understanding the text is a key career, college, and citizenship skill. However, teachers often worry that students will not read the assigned reading. Instead of trying to engage students in the reading, a teacher might enable students not to read by telling them the main points covered by the text. Many upper elementary, middle, and high school teachers express frustration about "not knowing how to get students to read." Again, the *Thinkquiry* tools—especially the collaborative routines—can help. Students enjoy using the collaborative routines to work through text with other students.

It is difficult to improve students' skills as readers, writers, and thinkers when they do not attempt to engage with text. In general, people do not improve their skills when they do not practice or use the skills they have. Therefore, it is important for all teachers to work with students in ways that support them to regularly read, write, and think critically and creatively in response to what they have read or learned. Using the *Thinkquiry* tools to help students engage with reading—print or online—and learning can be very helpful. Additionally, the more students use the *Thinkquiry* strategies, the more comfortable they become with using them—resulting in a more productive use of the strategies by students.

Strategies and Schema Matter!

Strategies. A good strategy enables students to approach and make meaning of a text or task in order to accomplish a goal. Selecting the right strategy can make the difference between not completing a task, completing a task at a minimal level of quality, and completing a task well.

It is important that students learn a variety of strategies and are able to select a good strategy to support a particular task. This ability to select and apply strategies is a skill that continues into college and career. Consider, for example, an employee who needs to advise his or her supervisor on the advantages and disadvantages of a particular product. If, on the one hand, the employee knows how to skim and scan and how to take good notes, he or she will be able to read a large amount of material in a short amount of time in order to be prepared to meet with the supervisor and give his or her informed opinion. If, on the other hand, the employee cannot skim and scan well and is not able to select the important points to capture in notes, he or she may not be able to complete the task well or on time.

Schema. Schema is background knowledge or prior knowledge related to the current task or topic. Humans tend to interpret what we see and encounter through a lens of what we already know. For example, it is much easier to understand a technical article about rare breeds of sheepdogs if you know something about sheep herding and something about dog breeding. If you know about neither of these, it will be a lot harder to understand and explain what you are reading.

In order to be college and career ready, students need to acquire deep knowledge in fewer areas, rather than shallow knowledge of many topics. This requires that students understand why something is important to know—and then spend enough time on the topic to learn it deeply. Students must make connections between what they are learning now with what they have studied previously, while building conceptual understanding and looking for patterns. In fact, this type of learning is what distinguishes novices from experts or those able to develop expertise. Whenever possible, teachers should support students in building knowledge from text, rather than frontloading the information. After reading and learning, students need to reflect on what they have learned and what questions they would still like to have answered. Reading and reflecting on a topic helps build schema and increases the capacity to learn more deeply on that topic.

Thinkquiry tools, such as **KWL Plus**, can help build schema and knowledge by providing students with strategies they can use as readers and learners to make meaning of the material.

How Do Schema and Strategies Work Together? Why Are They so Important When It Comes to Reading and Vocabulary Development?

Imagine that you have been away on vacation for the past week. When you return, there is a pile of mail. How do you deal with the mail most efficiently? You likely sort it quickly into piles. Perhaps your categories include junk mail, bills, personal mail, and catalogs or magazines that you want to save to read later.

Examples of cross-content area literacy skills include activating prior knowledge, setting a purpose for reading, clarifying, questioning, predicting, summarizing, visualizing, deductive and inductive thinking, brainstorming, and responding.

Sorting is a *strategy* to deal effectively with the challenge of a pile of mail. However, you did not sort the mail by color or size. You sorted by categories that you knew from prior experience would be useful to you. That is, you matched the *strategy* of sorting with the *purpose* of the task: handling the mail efficiently. From prior knowledge and experience of getting and opening mail, you recognize most types of mail and understand which types will likely be of interest to you. In other words, you have a *schema* for mail, an internal experience map that tells you how it is best to sort in order to accomplish your goal. If you do not have a good schema and a good strategy, you would have to open and read every piece of mail and decide what to do with it. This would take a very long time. If you were a poor reader—in addition to having no background knowledge and no strategy to handle the task—you might give up.

Now apply this scenario to reading comprehension and vocabulary development. If a reader has strategies for reading, she can match reading speed and approach to the purpose for reading. If she knows how and when it is helpful to skim and scan, summarize, code, and take notes, then she does not have to try to remember each word every time she reads a new text. If she has strategies for concept development, learning discipline-specific and technical vocabulary, and remembering academic terms, she does not have to try to memorize words and definitions. *That is why strategies and schema matter.*

Pulling It All Together: The Literacy Engagement and Instruction Cycle

Engagement and instruction are not an either/or proposition. Both are essential when it comes to improving student literacy and learning. If students are interested in what they are learning but lack skills to be independent readers, writers, and thinkers, then they rely heavily on the support of a teacher. If students have skills but are disengaged as readers and learners, their skills will not develop to sophisticated levels and teachers will have little opportunity to coach them to higher levels of proficiency.

> *Thinkquiry* tools use students' natural dispositions and help teachers motivate students to read, write, and think more deeply and with greater comprehension.

It might be helpful to think of the *Literacy Engagement and Instruction Cycle* as a coaching cycle. If teachers can get students on the field to play, then they can coach them to greater success. If students feel successful, then they are willing to continue playing. If they continue to play, then teachers can continue to coach.

Most students, as do most adults, like to make their own choices, interact with one another, set and meet goals, and do things for real reasons. The *Thinkquiry* tools take these dispositions and use them to engage students with print and electronic text. The *Thinkquiry* tools help teachers get students to read, write, and think more deeply and with greater comprehension.

The Literacy Engagement and Instruction Cycle

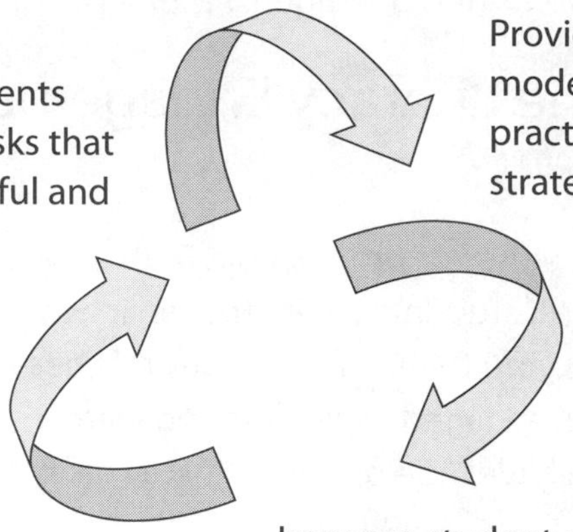

Engage students in literacy tasks that are meaningful and purposeful.

Provide instruction, modeling, and guided practice of literacy support strategies in context.

Improve student confidence, competence, and efficacy.

Figure 2.1: The Literacy Engagement Cycle

© Copyright 2008 Public Consulting Group

Electronic Text and the Use of *Thinkquiry* Tools

We know that many students will pay more attention and work harder if technology and media are involved. In addition, the sheer availability of accessible information and text on the Internet and open educational resources means that students—and their teachers—now have access to an amazing array of new resources that were previously inaccessible (for example, museum archives, current health information, up-to-date statistics, primary sources, scientific data of various types, and curriculum on many topics). This increases the opportunity to learn for everyone. We suggest that teachers build vocabulary and reading comprehension using technology and media where appropriate. Note that skillful use of electronic text and media may require additional instruction if they are to be maximized in the context of teaching and learning. Most students need instruction on how to assess bias, search for relevant information, read hypertext in a meaningful way, understand new online text structures, and evaluate source credibility.

> The key is supporting students to make connections between what they have already learned with what they are studying now, while building conceptual understanding and looking for patterns.

Many of the *Thinkquiry* reading comprehension and vocabulary tools are not only applicable but also important to use when working with electronic texts. Learning how to manage the information glut is a challenge. On a basic level, however, many of the same rules apply when reading electronic text as with print text. The reader needs to be able to make meaning of what is being read, practice reading multiple genres, understand the vocabulary, and combine text and vocabulary to deepen and extend understanding.

Technology can also assist students when using the strategies. Some examples of such strategies include marking or coding online text with color, highlighting or comments, using electronic templates when completing graphic organizers, posting **Quick Writes** to a blog site, or using a wiki when completing group summarizing. Each of these uses of technology can help students record individual or collaborative thinking; make editing, revising, and brainstorming easier; and increase students' active engagement when working to make meaning of print or electronic text.

> Vocabulary development is an integral part of content learning and is critical when students read and write about and discuss specific topics.

The Literacy Demands of Different Content Areas

Content literacy, sometimes called disciplinary literacy, is about

- How, what, and for what purposes students read and write in a particular content area
- How and why students speak and present in a given content area
- The types of thinking required by a specific discipline
- Applicable vocabulary, formats, and text structures

Some literacy skills are applicable to all disciplines. Students need to strategically read, write, speak, listen, present, and think within and across content areas. Examples of cross-content area literacy skills include activating prior knowledge, setting a purpose for reading, clarifying, questioning, predicting, summarizing, and responding.

There are also specific ways of reading, writing, speaking and listening, presenting, and thinking within each discipline that are particular to that discipline. For example, while primary sources and point of view are particularly important when studying history, so are experimentation and research important in science. Each discipline has its own particular text types and structures, presentation formats, conceptual vocabulary, and technical vocabulary. Many students need tools, strategies, and guided practice to become skilled readers, writers, and thinkers in the content areas. The following descriptions give examples of the literacy demands in four disciplines. Other disciplines, not represented here, share literacy demands similar to these, as well as having unique literacy needs.

Mathematics

Mathematics requires critical thinking, vocabulary and concept development, and the ability to learn from dense, concise text. The text challenges in the math classroom include word problems, textbook structures, proofs, articles, graphs, and charts. Mathematical language usage requires an understanding of operations, terminology that has precise meaning, and relevant conceptual vocabulary. Mathematical writing includes being able to write succinctly and clearly in various types of text: proofs, statistical analyses, response to problematic situations, notes combining symbols and text, and directions for solving problems and explanations.

Sample literacy tasks required of mathematics students

- Read dense explanatory text to better understand processes.

- Grasp abstract concepts and translate them into symbols.

- Distinguish and describe patterns.

- Decode words as well as numeric and non-numeric symbols.

- Translate words into problems and problems into words.

- Use journals to write about and examine ideas and reflect on solutions.

- Compare and contrast key concepts, record logic and proofs, and present solutions to multistep problems in writing.

Science

Science depends on reading and research skills, critical thinking and vocabulary, and concept development. Success in the science classroom requires skilled reading, skimming and scanning, and interpretation of a wide variety of genres and formats including articles, lab reports, textbooks, informational websites, graphs, charts, tables, and complex diagrams. Students use focused language in the study of science including process words, terminology with precise meanings, and conceptual vocabulary. Types of writing include lab reports, analytical essays, notes from text, demonstration, film and lecture, research projects, observational and procedural notes, summaries, and evidence-based conclusions.

Sample literacy tasks required of science students

- Compare and contrast concepts and ideas.

- Read concept-dense text accompanied by tables, graphs, and diagrams.

- Analyze and present data.

- Write careful and precise observations.

- Form hypotheses and draw conclusions.

- Understand how the specifics of a particular process or system relate to the bigger picture.

- Determine the relative importance and accuracy of information.

- Write about findings in learning logs or as part of lab report conclusions.

Social Studies/History

Social studies/history requires reading, critical thinking, vocabulary, concept development, and writing. When studying history and government, students need to be able to read and make sense of information from a wide variety of text formats including primary sources, textbooks, articles, nonfiction texts, maps, historical photographs, government documents, regulations, biographies, graphs, charts, and artifacts. Students need to be able to verbally summarize and debate, taking and defending a point of view. They need to be competent writers who can produce analytical essays, opinion essays, research projects, summaries, and evidence-based conclusions.

Sample literacy tasks required of social studies/history students

- Sequence and make connections between historical events.
- Understand text structures and features.
- Evaluate sources.
- Recognize issues and trends in context.
- Engage in reflective inquiry through reading and writing.
- Recognize and write about cause-and-effect relationships.
- Distinguish between, and write about, fact versus opinion.

English Language Arts

English language arts is heavily dependent on reading and writing. Literary genres and formats—poems, essays, short stories, plays, biographies, memoirs, novels, and letters—require a wide variety of reading approaches and skills. Language skills include grammar and conventions, technical vocabulary, and discipline-specific vocabulary, both the vocabulary of the discipline and the vocabulary of complex texts. Types of writing include opinion/argument, informational and expository, and narrative.

Sample literacy tasks required of English language arts students

- Articulate thinking orally and in writing for various audiences.
- Use grammar and conventions for precision and to convey meaning.
- Recognize and use rhetorical techniques.
- Define words and phrases in context.
- Recognize literary devices.
- Understand the structure of different genres.
- Use the writing process to plan, draft, revise, and edit writing that informs, argues, or tells a story.
- Recognize and delineate an author's claims, evidence, and reasoning.

The literacy requirements that cross disciplinary boundaries, as well as those unique to each discipline, are complex. They require modeling, practice, and scaffolding before students can master them on their own. These skills can be supported with the *Thinkquiry* tools and the *gradual release of responsibility model* (see the section on "Tips for Using the *Thinkquiry* Tools in Your Classroom").

The Connection between Vocabulary Development and Reading Comprehension

Vocabulary development is an integral part of content learning. We introduced Instructional Shift 1, Regular Practice with Complex Text and Its Academic Language, in Part 1 of this book; here, we'll give more detail relevant to *Thinkquiry* strategies. Vocabulary is key to learning content and concepts. If students do not know the meaning of the words and phrases in a text, they will have difficulty understanding the gist of the text, identifying key details, differentiating between terms, and communicating understanding with precision. Students learn vocabulary best in the context of the content being learned. Students need strategies to learn new vocabulary as well as opportunities to interact with new vocabulary multiple times in multiple ways so that they will retain it. When teachers use a variety of approaches to teach vocabulary, they notice that reading comprehension improves, as does the quality of student discussion and written work.

Vocabulary is a critical element in three aspects of reading comprehension:

1. Vocabulary allows the learner to make connections to prior knowledge and develop new knowledge.

2. Knowing the words they will encounter—and actively working to discern the meaning of unfamiliar words while reading—assists readers in understanding the text. When students understand 75–90 percent of the words they are reading, comprehension is typically adequate. If they understand fewer than 75 percent of the words that carry meaning in the text, it is difficult for students to make much sense of the text.

3. Developing an understanding of words needed to discuss and write about a topic allows students to think about and reflect on the topic, make connections, summarize, and draw conclusions. Students cannot be reflective about the content they are learning if they are not able to use the words associated with the content accurately and confidently. Actively working with the content they read creates new insights, allows students to develop robust understanding, and supports students as they build new knowledge—all critical elements of improving reading comprehension.

Different strategies and approaches work well depending on the types of words that students need to learn and the level of understanding that students need to have with the specific words. Students also may develop their own strategies for learning unfamiliar terms—strategies they can take with them into college and career where learning and remembering new words remain a lifelong endeavor. Because of the symbiotic relationship between vocabulary development and reading comprehension, it is productive to focus students' attention on words *before, during,* and *after* reading.

Table 2.1 lists three vocabulary learning challenges and specific *Thinkquiry* tools that can be used to address them.

Table 2.1: Vocabulary Learning Challenges and *Thinkquiry* Tools

Vocabulary Learning Challenge	*Thinkquiry* Tools
Developing conceptual understanding	Frayer Model, Word Sort, list-group-label
Learning and remembering discipline-specific terms (Tier 3)	Interactive Word Wall, Triple-Entry Vocabulary Journal, Semantic Feature Analysis, Knowledge Rating Guide
Learning and remembering academic vocabulary (Tier 2)	Word Analysis, Interactive Word Wall, Frayer Model, Knowledge Rating Guide

Knowing the vocabulary is one aspect of reading comprehension. Beyond the words, however, students must be able to make sense of the entirety of connected text. As students read more complex text, they need strategies to help them organize and process the information they are reading. According to Elaine McEwan's (2001) synthesis of the research, skilled readers are able to do the following on their own as needed with a variety of types of text:

- Activate prior knowledge
- Make text-based inferences
- Monitor comprehension
- Clarify understanding
- Question the text
- Search for and select pertinent information
- Summarize understanding
- Visualize when reading
- Organize content

Thinkquiry tools can help all students apply the skills of good readers to increasingly complex text. In each of the next sections of the Toolkit, there are collaborative routines that support students before, during, and after reading to make sense of and use what they have read. These collaborative routines provide scaffolding that works for all levels of readers and holds students responsible for learning and making meaning of text. Using the *Thinkquiry* tools frequently in the classroom will support students in vocabulary learning and reading comprehension.

Overview of the Research on Vocabulary Development and Reading Comprehension

The following is a brief summary of research[1] in the area of vocabulary development and reading comprehension. The summary highlights the key ideas that teachers will want to consider when planning and facilitating literacy-rich lessons and units that simultaneously increase content learning.

Thinkquiry tools specifically address best practices in vocabulary and reading comprehension. Classroom scenarios throughout the Toolkit illustrate what these tools look like "in action." Further information and research related to these key ideas and how they can be used in the upper elementary, middle, and high school classroom can be found in the Additional Resources at the end of this book.[2]

Vocabulary Development Research

Direct explicit instruction. Direct explicit instruction in vocabulary and learning from context are both important. Effective instruction includes description rather than definitions and word recognition through multiple interactions.

Strategies. Effective strategies include use of linguistic and nonlinguistic representations, gradual shaping of word meanings through multiple exposure, teaching and using word parts, using different types of instruction for different types of words, students' interaction with words, games, and a focus on academic terms.

Multiple interactions. Repetition, word work and word play, and teacher support are essential for increasing vocabulary.

Active engagement. Vocabulary learning should entail active engagement in learning tasks. Teach students to be independent word learners who know how to seek specific word meanings, appreciate multiple meanings of words, and enjoy using new words.

Reading Comprehension Research

Instructional considerations include

Time. Time spent reading and writing helps improve those skills.

Use of strategies. Particular literacy strategies—when explicitly taught, modeled, and practiced before, during, or after reading—enhance the ability of secondary students to read and write to learn across the content areas. More than 200 studies of comprehension strategy instruction, fourth grade and above, found evidence for the efficacy of comprehension monitoring, cooperative learning, graphic organizers, story structure, question generating, question answering, summarization, and the use of multiple strategies.

Keys to improved reading comprehension include

Meaningful context. Literacy skills and strategies should be taught in context whenever possible, not in isolation or as a worksheet activity.

Cross-content literacy. Content area teachers include modeling and literacy instruction embedded in the teaching of content so that students read and write like subject area experts.

Text-based collaborative learning. Instead of general classroom discussion, engage in specific analysis of text with students who have a wide range of abilities.

Use of diverse text. Part 1 of this book explains that in order to reach college and career readiness, all students must have the opportunity to read, listen to, discuss, and write about appropriately complex text. However, leveled text on a topic can serve as a scaffold to the vocabulary and concepts of more complex text. In addition, students benefit from reading diverse texts that present a wide range of topics and connect to students' cultural, linguistic, and demographic backgrounds.

Tips for Using *Thinkquiry* Tools in Your Classroom

In order for strategies and collaborative routines to become habits of practice for students, teachers must support them in developing expertise. In this section, we suggest several considerations for integrating *Thinkquiry* tools into content instruction on a regular basis.

Use the *Gradual Release of Responsibility Model* to Teach *Thinkquiry* Strategies Effectively

For *Thinkquiry* tools to be effective, research suggests using the *gradual release of responsibility model*. Teaching students how to use a *Thinkquiry* strategy is similar to coaching an athlete to improve his or her technique. A coach demonstrates (models), explains (explicitly describes and provides tips for how to approach the task), guides practice, and then asks the athlete to try the skill independently, providing feedback until the skill is mastered.

Teaching Thinkquiry strategies and collaborative routines is different from *assigning* them.

This same *gradual release of responsibility model* is helpful to use when teaching students a new learning strategy or collaborative routine. There are five steps in the *gradual release of responsibility model*:

1. **Pre-assessment.** Think about what types of literacy habits and skills are necessary to be successful on the assigned task and the level of support that students will need. Then select an appropriate *Thinkquiry* strategy, collaborative routine, or instructional practice to use with students. Before teaching students how to use the tool, check to see if students know the approach or if they have done it in the past.

2. **Explicit instruction and modeling.** Provide explicit directions and *model* how to use the strategy or complete the collaborative routine. *Modeling* means demonstrating how to go about completing a task using the same strategy students will use. For example, to model the **Coding** strategy (see Part 4) the teacher might read the beginning of the text with students and model each of the codes. During modeling, it is important to clarify expectations for quality and suggest tips for successful completion of a task using the approach.

3. **Guided practice.** Ask students to practice the strategy in pairs or small groups and provide ample feedback along the way so that students know whether they are on track or not. Ask students to reflect on how the strategy, collaborative routine, or instructional support is affecting their reading and learning.

4. **Independent practice.** Ask students to practice the approach on their own with content and levels of challenge similar to what they practiced in groups or pairs. Be sure to provide feedback, or have students provide feedback for one another.

5. **Independent application and transfer.** Ask students to apply the strategy or collaborative routine to other situations and contexts.

Match the Right *Thinkquiry* Tool to the Type of Text You Ask Students to Read

Content teachers often find it challenging to help students read and comprehend complex texts in their disciplines. They may attribute this challenge to not knowing how to teach reading. Yet, as discussed in Part 1, the content teacher is the teacher who knows the most about the literacy demands of his or her discipline and can support students in navigating, discussing, and writing about text in the content area.

The key to supporting students in reading content area text lies in asking and answering three questions about a text: What is my learning goal? What about this text might be difficult for my students? Which strategies or tools will work best to help students navigate the challenges this text presents?

1. What is the learning goal?

The first step is being clear what students must learn or do with the text. Teachers often identify a content learning goal first. For example:

- I want my students to read the chapter to learn what happened during the Second Continental Congress.
- I want my students to read the handout and understand the difference between erosion and weathering.
- My students need to know the different ways to solve quadratic equations explained at the beginning of chapter 8.

Additionally, there will be a learning goal or goals addressing a literacy standard. Once the learning goals are clear, it is easier to select (or adapt) a *Thinkquiry* tool.

Here are two examples of combined content and literacy goals and the *Thinkquiry* tools that could support them:

- Connect events in our nation's past to conflicts today

  Discussion Web, Coding/Comprehension Monitoring, Venn diagram, Analytic Graphic Organizer, Save the Last Word for Me
- Compare and contrast two natural processes

  Group Summarizing, Jigsaw, Discussion Web, Coding/ Comprehension Monitoring, Picture This!

Thinkquiry tools provide a bridge and a support for students as they learn to do complex academic tasks.

2. What might be difficult about this text for students?

In Part 1 of *Thinkquiry,* we introduced the concept of text complexity and discussed both quantitative and qualitative factors. However, teachers do not always recognize the qualitative complexity of a particular text because it is a type of text or a topic with which they, themselves, are familiar. For example, a science teacher may be so comfortable with reading science texts that it seems like second nature. Because reading scientific content without difficulty is commonplace for science teachers, it may be difficult for teachers to envision what students will struggle with in the text. However, in order to support students in reading and comprehending any text, it is important to try to look at the text as a novice and to analyze its cognitive demands for students.

> In order to scaffold students to read effectively, it is critical to try to look at the text as an outsider and to analyze its cognitive demands.

There are several things a teacher can consider when thinking about what might make a text difficult for students. Fisher, Frey, and Lapp (2009) define four categories:

- Comprehension challenges
- Vocabulary challenges
- Complex text structure
- Multiple text features

Comprehension challenges. A student's ability or inability to comprehend a text can be affected by three factors: (1) the reader's background knowledge (or lack thereof), (2) the density of the text (for example, if paragraphs are packed with complicated ideas with little explanation or if the text is very abstract), and (3) the reader's ability to read strategically.

Most of us have read an article or a book and have come across a paragraph, section, or chapter that did not make sense. This happens frequently when a reader has little background knowledge about a topic. For example, a reader familiar with motorcycles can read and understand a more challenging text about motorcycles than can someone who knows little about them.

Limited comprehension can also occur when the text is unusually dense or unfamiliar. Textbooks, primary sources, and research reports are examples of text types that are challenging for some readers because the ideas are packed so tightly.

Lastly, the skill of the reader is a factor. When readers have limited "strategic and active moves" needed to understand a text or parts of it, they often "slide words" in front of their eyes but do not comprehend what they read. These readers may not be in the habit of questioning the text, rereading, adjusting reading speed to purpose and challenge, identifying key words and using word-solving strategies, or annotating or diagramming as they read—all strategies that good readers use to make sense of complex text.

> Readers may not be in the habit of questioning the text, rereading, adjusting speed, identifying key words, using word-solving strategies, or annotating as they read—all strategies that good readers use to make sense of complex text.

As teachers consider the comprehension challenges involved with a specific piece of text, they need to think about the background knowledge of the students, the relative density of the text, and reading skills students may or may not already have.

Vocabulary, text structure, and text features. Beyond the comprehension factors mentioned previously (background knowledge, text density, and students' ability to read strategically) three other factors interfere with comprehension. Vocabulary, as discussed earlier, text structures—the way a text is organized—and text features all play a part in making a text easier or more challenging for students.

Here are some examples of how these factors can make a text challenging to read and understand: A biography of a sports figure is usually set up in chronological order. This is typically easy for the reader to understand. However, depending on the sport being discussed (for example, rugby, lacrosse, cricket, curling), a reader unfamiliar with these sports might struggle to understand the vocabulary, the rules of the sport, or the context of the events being described. On the other hand, the vocabulary of a novel may be fairly familiar to students, but the events may be described in a stream-of-consciousness or nonlinear way that makes it challenging to determine the order of events (for example, *Catch 22, The House on Mango Street*). Finally, although graphic novels are compelling to look at, their unique text features make understanding the narrative extremely difficult for many readers. So, too, the callouts and added graphics in some technical articles that are intended as a vital part of the articles' content are features that either confuse readers, or readers just ignore them.

As teachers choose texts for their own classes, they need to consider the qualitative challenges the texts might present for the students who are reading them. Table 2.2 presents some questions teachers can ask themselves to provide a starting place for analysis.

Table 2.2: Questions Teachers Can Ask Themselves

Text Complexity Challenge	Questions Teachers Can Ask Themselves about the Text
Comprehension	1. Is the text fiction or nonfiction? 2. Are there areas that seem to be particularly dense (information-packed)? 3. Is this a topic with which your students are familiar? 4. What strategic reading skills do your students have or need to understand this text?
Vocabulary	1. What are the important discipline-specific terms (Tier 3), for example, *anemone, bifurcation, quadratic equation*? 2. What are the important general academic words (Tier 2), for example, *process, system, independent, research, proposition, concept*?
Text Structure	1. How is the text organized? Is there an introduction followed by sections with a main idea and examples? Are there stanzas? Are ideas compared and contrasted within the text? Are there places where the author makes a claim? Are there sections of the text that describe cause and effect? 2. Is there a single structure throughout the text or many substructures to the text? 3. Is the text chronological in nature? Does it have tangents? Are there flashbacks?

Text Features	1. Is there information in photos or drawings that students will need to understand?
	2. What types of graphs, tables, diagrams, or maps are present? Will students need support to read them?
	3. Are there terms in bold that will help students understand the text?
	4. Are there features that will distract them?
	5. How are the features of this text different from others students have read?

3. Which strategies or tools are best suited to address the challenges this text presents?

Once teachers have identified potential challenges for their students, how can they use that knowledge to plan and teach in a way that will support students? Here are three ways to use *Thinkquiry* tools to help students comprehend complex text:

- Choose instructional practices to help students work around the challenges in the text.
- Model and teach strategies for dealing with the challenges in the text.
- Differentiate support for students who need it.

The first way to support students in comprehending challenging content area text is to make use of **instructional practices** that help scaffold their learning. These are located in each section of *Thinkquiry Toolkit 1*. For instance, if students need to build background knowledge in order to comprehend the text, the appropriate tools are found in Part 3, Laying the Foundation. An **Anticipation/Reaction Guide** or an **Interactive Word Wall** will help introduce important concepts. A **Word Sort** or a **Small Group Vocabulary Preview** introduce key vocabulary. The key to selecting the right strategies and practices is to first identify the challenges and then match them with a tool that helps meet those challenges.

In addition to using instructional practices that provide direct support for students, it is important to model and teach strategies students can learn to use independently during reading. Model the use of a **Triple-Entry Vocabulary Journal** that students will keep during reading. Provide and model the use of **Analytic Graphic Organizers** to help students organize and bring clarity to text structures. **Paired Reading** is an excellent strategy students can use to work together to digest more complex texts.

When all students are reading the same text, the cognitive load of the text can be adjusted by the task required of students. For example, a group of highly able readers may use an analytical strategy when reading, while a group of less able readers may use a summarizing strategy. Instead of using different strategies, all students may use the same strategy with the template differentiated, for example, **Two-Column Note Taking**, with different headings. When **Coding** the text, some students may use different codes than others to note more concrete or more abstract concepts. Regardless of which strategy students use, it is important for the teacher to **support students** in learning the strategy through a *gradual release of responsibility model*. In order for students to use a strategy independently, they must first learn to use it with support.

Differentiate literacy support—strategically provide parallel texts for varying reading abilities. The reality is that there are often students with widely different reading abilities in the same class. For some topics, tasks, or activities, it makes sense to provide parallel texts of different complexity for students who read above or below the level of the core text. The advantage to doing this is that all students will be able to think critically about the ideas being presented and to engage in high-level discussion about content. By reading easier or more challenging texts, all students have an appropriate entry point into full participation. However, it is critical to keep in mind that a primary goal of the CCSS in ELA & Literacy is for all students to independently read and comprehend appropriately complex text. While it may be necessary to differentiate reading levels to help students learn and discuss content, students cannot be in leveled text all the time. They need to encounter challenging texts and be supported in a variety of ways to help them gain independence in reading those texts.

Designing Lesson Plans That Increase Content Learning

Planning—and implementing—engaging, rigorous lessons that support both content learning and literacy development is not easy, especially for teachers who are just beginning to integrate literacy into instruction. There are many considerations. In order to integrate literacy instruction effectively into the learning of content, a teacher must choose both the content standards and the literacy standards that are the learning targets for a lesson or unit. The teacher will also need to think about the texts that students will read as part of the unit—and the challenges that each text presents to readers. Then the teacher will choose instructional practices, student learning strategies, and collaborative routines that will be most effective in helping students to think deeply about the content using the selected texts.

It is also important to plan assignments and tasks that engage students and help accomplish learning goals. For students to become effective content area readers, writers, and thinkers, they need to complete assignments that build their literacy and learning skills and support content learning (Irvin, Meltzer, Mickler, Phillips, & Dean, 2009).

Assignments should also engage and motivate students. Students need to know the purpose of a task and understand how it relates to the goals of the unit or lesson. Rigor is an important consideration as well. If an assignment is too easy or too hard, it will not be engaging. Approaches to improved student engagement with content include

- Establishing an authentic reason to read or write
- Reading or writing in conjunction with hands-on activities
- Using collaborative learning routines

Student success with content area reading and writing assignments depends on the quality of the literacy instruction that supports learning. Reading and writing assignments should include (Irvin et al., 2009)

- Clear instructions, criteria, and examples of quality assignment responses to ensure that students know the expectations, including a rubric for assessment

- Content area reading or writing instruction within the context of completing the assignment (for example, modeling of strategies, brainstorming of approaches, analysis of exemplars or rubrics)
- Coaching and feedback throughout that allows students to improve their comprehension and quality of work (for example, use of the writing process, peer editing, paired reading, use of the assessment rubric prior to developing a final draft)

Supporting student success when in content reading and writing takes time, planning, and practice, but the benefits to students and their learning are well worth the effort. The following template can be used when planning content literacy instruction.

Content Literacy Planning Template

Grade Level/Content Area/Unit Topic	
Learning Standards	
Content What specific content or concepts will students know, understand, and be able to apply? Questions to Think About • When students ask why they need to know this content, what is the answer? • How will students be exposed to and investigate this content? • What prior knowledge do students need? • What connections can be made to other content within and across content areas and to real-life applications? • What vocabulary will be essential to understanding the target concepts? How will students learn this?	
Literacy Habits and Skills	
Literacy Outcomes How will students read, write, discuss, present, and engage in critical and creative thinking in relation to the content? Questions to Think About • What, specifically, will students be expected to read? To write? To discuss? To present? • How will students engage in critical thinking (analysis, evaluation) and/or creative thinking (innovative application, synthesis)? • What modeling or explicit teaching will be necessary? • What literacy strategies do students know that they could apply to the tasks at hand? • How will students get feedback and coaching along the way?	

Content Literacy Planning Template (*continued*)

Grade Level/Content Area/Unit Topic	
Meeting Adolescent Learning Needs	
Motivation and Engagement How will structured or supported choice, use of technology, collaborative learning, and authentic reasons to read and write be a part of the learning of this content?	
Questions to Think About • Which strategies will motivate or engage students? • What differentiation may be needed?	
Assessment/Grading	
Quality Improvement How will rubrics, exemplars, and clear expectations provide guidance for the processes students will demonstrate and the products they will produce? • Are the grading criteria clearly stated in the language of the standards and learning targets? • How will students receive actionable feedback?	
Resources	
Specific Texts and Materials/Technology/People Resources Needed to Support Success	
Notes Related to Facilitation of Instruction	

Evaluating Classroom Practice

When starting to incorporate literacy practices into a content area, some teachers may find it helpful to assess their current classroom practices for areas of personal strengths and challenges related to integrating literacy and content learning.

Here's how:

1. Read through the rubric and complete the ratings.

2. Select two or three areas for improvement.

3. For those areas, look through *Thinkquiry Toolkit 1* to identify some possible strategies. List these and check periodically to make sure you are using the tools productively and frequently.

4. At the end of the year, return to the areas for improvement selected during the self-assessment and complete the ratings again.

Teacher Self-Assessment Rubric

Directions

Complete each individual component of the Teacher Self-Assessment Rubric (CCSSO) by selecting the levels of frequency and proficiency that best describe your use of literacy best practices and instructional strategies to support student learning within your content area.

Frequency

1. I don't use this best practice.
2. I occasionally use this best practice.
3. I frequently use this best practice during a lesson or unit.
4. I consistently use this best practice during a lesson or unit.

Proficiency

1. I don't understand this literacy best practice or how to implement it in my classroom.
2. This best practice is familiar, but I would benefit from seeing it in action in my content area.
3. I am confident that the way I implement this best practice supports improved student learning in my classroom.
4. I am extremely confident when implementing this best practice and believe my use of this practice could serve as a model for others.

In the last column of the rubric, indicate the *Thinkquiry* tools you could use that support more frequent implementation of this practice.

Teacher Self-Assessment Rubric (*continued*)

Literacy Component	Self-Assessment	*Thinkquiry* Tools That Support This Practice
Vocabulary Development		
Word-Rich Environment I support students as they learn new content vocabulary by using a variety of strategies to create a word-rich environment.	Frequency ① ② ③ ④ Proficiency ① ② ③ ④	
Explicit Instruction I teach students how to use strategies to: • Connect new words to prior knowledge • Generate definitions from contextual cues and word analysis • Organize new words around core concepts	Frequency ① ② ③ ④ Proficiency ① ② ③ ④	
Repeated Opportunities to Interact with Words I provide students with multiple opportunities to connect with, use, and remember content vocabulary.	Frequency ① ② ③ ④ Proficiency ① ② ③ ④	

Frequency

1. I don't use this best practice.
2. I occasionally use this best practice.
3. I frequently use this best practice during a lesson or unit.
4. I consistently use this best practice during a lesson or unit.

Proficiency

1. I don't understand this literacy best practice or how to implement it in my classroom.
2. This best practice is familiar, but I would benefit from seeing it in action in my content area.
3. I am confident that the way I implement this best practice supports improved student learning in my classroom.
4. I am extremely confident when implementing this best practice and believe my use of this practice could serve as a model for others.

Teacher Self-Assessment Rubric (*continued*)

Literacy Component	Self-Assessment	*Thinkquiry* Tools That Support This Practice
Reading Comprehension		
Use of High Impact *before* Reading Strategies I teach and provide opportunities for students to use the following specific strategies to support their readiness for reading tasks: • Activating prior knowledge • Setting a purpose for reading	Frequency ① ② ③ ④ Proficiency ① ② ③ ④	
Use of High Impact *during* Reading Strategies I teach and provide opportunities for students to use the following specific strategies to improve comprehension during reading: • Identifying main ideas and supporting details or evidence by annotating or marking the text • Analyzing information by identifying fact, opinion, point of view, bias, and generalizations • Asking questions to interact with text • Making inferences and drawing conclusions • Visualizing events, actions, relationships, and/or patterns	Frequency ① ② ③ ④ Proficiency ① ② ③ ④	
Use of High Impact *after* Reading Strategies I teach and provide opportunities for students to use the following specific strategies to help them respond to text after reading: • Reflecting about information and ideas in text • Using writing frequently in conjunction with reading • Summarizing information and concepts	Frequency ① ② ③ ④	
• Synthesizing ideas and information to enable transfer of concepts to new applications and situations	Proficiency ① ② ③ ④	

Teacher Self-Assessment Rubric (*continued*)

Literacy Component	Self-Assessment	*Thinkquiry* Tools That Support This Practice
Reading Comprehension		
Student-Centered Discussion I provide opportunities for students to discuss and share their understanding of content area texts through the use of strategies that encourage collaborative analysis, inquiry, and deep discussion.	Frequency ① ② ③ ④ Proficiency ① ② ③ ④	
Wide Reading I expect students to engage in reading a variety of types of content area texts, including electronic text/media, and I provide in-class opportunities and resources for them to read.	Frequency ① ② ③ ④ Proficiency ① ② ③ ④	
Text Structure and Organization I support students in recognizing the organization and patterns of text structure in order to support understanding of content, especially when I assign a new type of text (for example, article, short story, textbook, word problem, graph, chart, or electronic text/media).	Frequency ① ② ③ ④ Proficiency ① ② ③ ④	
Gradual Release of Responsibility I help students transfer reading comprehension skills and strategies for independent use through a process of gradual release. The *gradual release of responsibility model* includes these steps: • Explicit teacher instruction and modeling • Guided small-group practice • Individual student practice with feedback • Independent application by each student	Frequency ① ② ③ ④ Proficiency ① ② ③ ④	

Frequency	Proficiency
1. I don't use this best practice.	1. I don't understand this literacy best practice or how to implement it in my classroom.
2. I occasionally use this best practice.	2. This best practice is familiar, but I would benefit from seeing it in action in my content area.
3. I frequently use this best practice during a lesson or unit.	3. I am confident that the way I implement this best practice supports improved student learning in my classroom.
4. I consistently use this best practice during a lesson or unit.	4. I am extremely confident when implementing this best practice and believe my use of this practice could serve as a model for others.

Notes

1. For specific research citations, please refer to the References at the end of this book.

2. You may also want to reference the *Time to Act* (2009) report issued by the Carnegie Corporation of New York.

PART 3: Laying the Foundation *before* Reading/Learning

Introduction

Activating prior knowledge and building background knowledge prepares and motivates students to read and learn. You can prepare students to read and learn by helping them identify what they already know and checking in on their current understanding of the topic at hand. Then you can plan your instruction to remedy misconceptions, build on existing knowledge, and avoid repeating information that students already know.

In Part 3 of the Toolkit, you will find student learning strategies, a collaborative routine, and teacher instructional practices, all of which will help students interact with vocabulary and text before reading and learning. Many of these tools can also be used throughout the reading and learning process to support understanding.

Helping students to reflect throughout reading and learning builds metacognition. Metacognition allows students to think about the strategies they are using to accomplish a particular task. Developing metacognition strengthens learning skills and builds confidence. You can use the *Thinkquiry* tools in this section to guide students to reflect on their thinking. The tools prompt students to ask—and answer—questions such as: What do I know? What do I need to know? What do I need to do? How can I do this? How well did it work? What did I learn? What can I do better next time?

In this section of the Toolkit, you will find the following approaches to supporting reading and learning:

	Reading and Learning Phases		
	Before	During	After
Student Learning Strategies			
Knowledge Rating Guide	✓	✓	✓
Frayer Model	✓		✓
Triple-Entry Vocabulary Journal	✓	✓	✓
Word Sort	✓		✓
Word Analysis	✓	✓	
KWL Plus	✓	✓	✓
Quick Write	✓	✓	✓
Collaborative Routine			
Partner/Small Group Vocabulary Preview	✓		
Teacher Practices			
Interactive Word Wall	✓	✓	✓
Chapter Preview/Tour	✓		
Anticipation/Reaction Guide	✓	✓	✓
Classroom Scenario			
Use of *Triple-Entry Vocabulary Journal* in a High School Science Classroom	✓	✓	✓

Knowledge Rating Guide

Description

A **Knowledge Rating Guide** is a *before, during,* and *after* reading activity in which students analyze their understanding of vocabulary words or concepts from the text or unit of study (Blachowicz, 1986).

Common Core Connection	Shift
When using a **Knowledge Rating Guide** with Tier 2 academic vocabulary, be sure to write the term in context (embedded in the sentence or phrase as it appears in the text), rather than alone. Tier 2 words may vary in meaning depending on the context.	1

Purpose

Use *before* reading to

- Introduce a list of key terms to students.
- Determine students' knowledge of a word or concept.
- Activate existing background knowledge.
- Help students make connections to new concepts.
- Assess learning when used *before* and *after* reading.

Directions

1. Select a list of important terms from the text. Prepare a handout that lists the terms followed by three columns: *Know It/Use It, Can Describe It/Don't Use It, Don't Know It/Don't Use It.*

Term	Know It/Use It	Can Describe It/Don't Use It	Don't Know It/Don't Use It

2. Give the **Knowledge Rating Guide** with the terms to students. Ask each student to rate his or her level of knowledge about each term by placing an X in the appropriate column.

3. Place students in small groups to talk about the terms and/or lead the class in a discussion about the terms that students know.

4. Ask students to read the text.

5. After reading the text, have students reexamine their sheets and see what words they can now define or use.

Extensions

Ask students to write down definitions or explanations of the terms they marked in the *Know It/Use It* column.

Before discussing the terms as a class, have members of each small group discuss the terms and explain them to one another; only discuss as a class the terms that no one knows.

Knowledge Rating Guide Template

Name: _____

Date: _____

Term	Know It/Use It 👍	Can Describe It/Don't Use It ✋	Don't Know It/Don't Use It 👎

Knowledge Rating Guide Content Examples

Mathematics

Elementary School

During a unit on geometry exploration, have students use a **Knowledge Rating Guide** description to help students monitor their understanding of key vocabulary words.

Term	Know It/Use It 👍	Can Describe It/Don't Use It ✋	Don't Know It/Don't Use It 👎
Congruent		✓	
Polygon		✓	
Attributes			✓

Middle School

Before a unit on ratio, proportion, and percent, give students a **Knowledge Rating Guide** description sheet with key mathematical terms they need to know at the end of the unit. Have them fill out the chart to assess their current understanding. For every term they do know, have them record their own definitions in their math journals. Re-administer the guide later in the unit to assess growth with respect to vocabulary.

Term	Know It/Use It	Can Describe It/Don't Use It	Don't Know It/Don't Use It
Ratio			
Percent			
Fraction			

High School

Before studying a unit on number theory in an integrated math class, provide students with a **Knowledge Rating Guide** template with terms for a quick assessment of their understanding. For each of the terms students do not know, have them keep a **Triple-Entry Vocabulary Journal** as a personal vocabulary list. Assess students on their understanding of their personal terms throughout the unit.

Term	Know It/Use It	Can Describe It/Don't Use It	Don't Know It/Don't Use It
Real numbers			
Natural numbers			
Integers			
Rational numbers			
Irrational numbers			
Prime numbers			
Repeating numbers			

Science

The science examples here were created for the same topic across the three grade spans for one strand in physics: motion.

Elementary School

Before a series of lessons on motion, distribute the following **Knowledge Rating Guide**.

Term	Know It/Use It 👍	Can Describe It/Don't Use It ✋	Don't Know It/Don't Use It 👎
Push			
Pull			
Force			
Direction			

Middle School

Use a similar template at the middle school level before starting a unit on motion.

Term	Know It/Use It	Can Describe It/Don't Use It	Don't Know It/Don't Use It
Force			
Friction			
Inertia			
Gravitational force			

High School

Challenge students to understand motion by studying the physics of driving a car. Incorporate concepts such as the distance traveled during braking at different speeds, the time required to stop at a changing traffic light, centripetal force on banked curves, and the science of skidding. Engage students at the beginning of the unit by including both core physics terms, as well as a few terms related to the context of the unit.

Term	Know It/Use It	Can Describe It/Don't Use It	Don't Know It/Don't Use It
Speed			
Acceleration			
Stopping distance			
Velocity			
Centripetal force			
Front-wheel drive			

Social Studies

Elementary School

Use to develop an understanding of students' prior knowledge when studying the geography of the United States.

Term	Know Where It Is 👍	Have Heard of It ✋	Never Heard of It 👎
Mississippi River			
Rocky Mountains			
Everglades			

Middle School

Use to build an understanding of specific terms related to the study of ancient Mesopotamia.

Term	Know It Well	Sort of Know It	Don't Know It
Cuneiform			
Stylus			
Ziggurat			

High School

Use as a review strategy to identify students' level of familiarity with specific technical terms before taking an exam on United States constitutional law.

Term	Can Define It	Have Heard of It	Never Heard of It
Habeas corpus			
Article			
Amendment			
Ratify			

English Language Arts

Elementary School

Use to access students' prior knowledge of basic literary terms.

Term	Know It/Use It 👍	Can Describe It/Don't Use It ✋	Don't Know It/Don't Use It 👎
Point of view			
Conflict			
Plot			

Middle School

Use to help students assess their own understanding of critical academic skills.

Term	Know It/Use It	Can Describe It/Don't Use It	Don't Know It/Don't Use It
Infer			
Analyze			
Synthesize			

High School

Use to access prior understanding of terms used in the study of poetry.

Term	Know It/Use It	Can Describe It/Don't Use It	Don't Know It/Don't Use It
Couplet			
Blank verse			
Sonnet			

Frayer Model

Description

A **Frayer Model** is a graphic organizer that helps students gain a more sophisticated understanding of vocabulary by using four quadrants on a chart to define examples, nonexamples, characteristics, and noncharacteristics of a word or concept (Frayer & Klausmeier, 1969).

Common Core Connection	Instructional Shift
The **Frayer Model** is valuable for building deep knowledge of a key concept. It is useful for helping students categorize and differentiate among terms that may be confusing or for which the definition may be complex. The Frayer Model can be an excellent formative assessment tool, used before and after reading about a concept.	1

Purpose

Use *before* or *after* reading to

- Help students form a better understanding of abstract terms or concepts that are easily confused.

  Help students differentiate between a definition of a concept or vocabulary word and those characteristics that are associated with it.

Directions

1. Select the word or concept to be defined using the **Frayer Model**.
2. Show the **Frayer Model** and explain the four quadrants.
3. Model how to use the **Frayer Model** to define a concept, using a simple example that students can understand.
4. Have students brainstorm a list of words and ideas related to the concept and then work together to complete the **Frayer Model**. Students may need to use a dictionary or glossary for clues.
5. Have students create a definition of the concept in their own words.

Extensions

Describe the rationale for examples and nonexamples.

Use the **Frayer Model** as a note-taking strategy during reading.

Change the titles of the boxes to include concept development categories, such as etymology.

Frayer Model Example

Example of a **Frayer Model** Graphic Organizer.

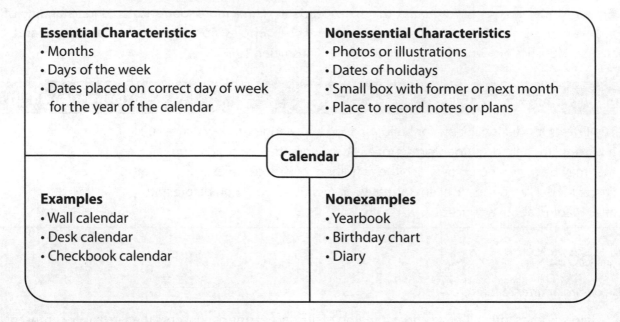

Essential Characteristics
- Months
- Days of the week
- Dates placed on correct day of week for the year of the calendar

Nonessential Characteristics
- Photos or illustrations
- Dates of holidays
- Small box with former or next month
- Place to record notes or plans

Calendar

Examples
- Wall calendar
- Desk calendar
- Checkbook calendar

Nonexamples
- Yearbook
- Birthday chart
- Diary

Frayer Model Template

Name: _____

Date: _____

Directions

Place the concept to be defined in the center square of the chart. Brainstorm a list of all of the words you know that relate to the word or concept. Classify all of the brainstormed words into one of the four boxes in the chart. Use the information to write a definition of the concept.

Brainstorming List

Essential Characteristics   Nonessential Characteristics

Examples   Nonexamples

Definition

Frayer Model Content Examples

English Language Arts

During and *after* reading a novel.

Have students identify a literary device used in their novels, such as figurative language, symbols, or personification. On poster board, students write the device in the center of a **Frayer Model** template and complete the four quadrants, leading to a definition of the literary device. Post the charts around the classroom to remind students of the literary devices that can be used when writing.

Mathematics

Before, during, and *after* reading the first chapter on coordinates and directed line segments in the complex textbook for analytic geometry.

Initiate a class practice of creating **Frayer Model** examples of analytic geometry terms that can be duplicated and kept in the front of students' math notebooks, starting with the easier terms that were taught in earlier math courses. Have students work in small groups to create definitions of the key terms, such *as real numbers, rational numbers, periodic decimals, line segments,* and *coordinates.* Gradually have students become independent in creating Frayer Model definitions of essential course concepts.

Science

Before and *after* a high school physics lesson sequence that teaches students about the concept of acceleration.

Early in the class, inform students that they will be creating a **Frayer Model** for a term that has both a common as well as a very specific scientific meaning. Work with students to create a Frayer Model for the term *acceleration.*

Toward the end of the lesson sequence, have students work in pairs to revisit their original Frayer Models for the term *acceleration* and highlight any ideas that have changed. Then have them create a new Frayer Model that demonstrates their new understanding of the scientific meaning of the term.

Social Studies

Before, during, and *after* reading about and taking a self-assessment of personality styles in a psychology course.

Have each student create a **Frayer Model** about his or her personality style that was revealed in the self-assessment, working alone or with others of the same style, as they prefer. Then, group students with different styles together to share their Frayer Models and explain their differing traits and behaviors.

Triple-Entry Vocabulary Journal

Description

The **Triple-Entry Vocabulary Journal** is a strategy for learning new vocabulary that uses a three-column note-taking format with columns for a word in context, the definition in one's own words, and a picture, memory aid, or phrase related to the word.

Common Core Connection	Instructional Shift
Defining vocabulary in context is an important component of close reading. The **Triple-Entry Vocabulary Journal** will help students remember words they have defined in context.	1

Purpose

Use *before, during,* and *after* reading to

- Help students understand key words when reading text.
- Provide an interactive way to learn new vocabulary.
- Provide a way for students to cognitively process new words, resulting in more retention.
- Help students develop a customized glossary to the text that provides words in context, applicable definitions, and personalized memory or study aids.

Directions

1. Determine the key words students should understand while reading a selection.
2. Have students divide a notebook page into three columns. Label the columns as follows: *Word in Context; Definition in My Own Words; Picture, Memory Aid, or Phrase.*
3. Model the strategy with several words.
   - In the first column, write down the sentence(s) within which the word is found, and underline or circle the word. Note the page on which you found the word.
   - Look up the word in the dictionary. Choose the meaning that fits the context of the word in your text. Write down a definition of the word in your own words in the second column.
   - In the third column, draw an image, jot a phrase, or create a memory device that will help you remember the word and its meaning.
   - Have students practice the strategy, sharing their definitions and memory aids.

Extensions

Have students select words they don't know while reading. Assign a predetermined number of total words and/or how many words per page/section/chapter the student should select to enter in the **Triple-Entry Vocabulary Journal** for each reading selection.

Jigsaw the word list to be found in a particular section of text and distribute different words to different students in small groups. Students then look through the text for the words before reading the selection to find the words, write them in the context of the sentence, and complete the strategy. Then students in each group discuss and teach one another the words they will need to know for the text they are going to read.

Have students compare and contrast one another's responses and discuss the words they found and did not know, supporting the development of word knowledge.

Triple-Entry Vocabulary Journal Template

Name: _____

Date: _____

Word in Context	Definition in My Own Words	Picture, Memory Aid, or Phrase

Triple-Entry Vocabulary Journal Content Examples

Mathematics

Elementary School

During a unit on the number system, use **Triple-Entry Vocabulary Journal** entries to show how to use place values to read numbers.

Word in Context	Your Definition	Your Memory Aid
The **ones period** includes ones, tens, and hundreds.	A set of small numbers starting with 1 that goes up to 999	**1, 10, 100,** 9,999
The **thousands period** includes one thousands, ten thousands, and hundred thousands.	A set of bigger numbers starting from 1,000 to up a million	**1,**000, **10,**000, **100,**000, 999,999
The **millions period** includes one millions, ten millions, and hundred millions.	A set of really big numbers starting from 1 million up to a billion	**1,**000,000, **10,**000,000 **100,**000,000, 999,999,999

Middle School

When reviewing fractions and equivalents, use **Triple-Entry Vocabulary Journal** entries to help students remember the meanings of the related math terms.

Word in Context	Your Definition	Your Memory Aid
A **fraction** is the name of a part of a whole or a part of a set.	A part of something whose size is shown by a number	Pizza cut into slices
The **denominator** of the fraction shows the number of parts of the whole set.	The bottom number in a fraction that shows how many total parts there are	All 8 slices in a pizza pie
The **numerator** of the fraction shows the number of parts under consideration.	The top number in a fraction that shows the portion	2/8 means 2 slices of a pizza that is cut into 8 slices

High School

Use **Triple-Entry Vocabulary Journal** entries to record terminology when studying interest during a financial management unit.

Word in Context	Your Definition	Your Memory Aid
Simple interest is equal to the principal (amount loaned) times the rate (percent of interest charged) times time (number of years the money is loaned). I = PRT	When money is borrowed, a person must pay back the amount borrowed, plus an additional percentage.	If I borrow $20,000 to buy a car at 5% for 5 years, the total for the car is $20,000 plus $1,000 (.05 x 20,000) each year = $25,000 total.
Compound interest is interest paid on the principal plus the interest added to date. It can be compounded annually, semi-annually, quarterly, monthly, or daily.	When money is saved, a person gets an extra amount of money called interest that compounds, or grows, bigger over time, as new interest is paid on the principal and all of the previous interest.	Saving $1,000 at 5% interest for 25 years at simple interest, I get $50/year or $2,250 total. With compound interest, I get interest on the interest = $3,386.35 in 25 years.

Science

Elementary School

Before a science lab about light, have small groups work together to define key terms.

Word in Context	Your Definition	Your Memory Aid
Shine a flashlight on clear glass, which is **transparent**. It lets light go through it so that you see what's on the other side.	Transparent means you can see through it clearly.	A view from a window on a sunny day
Fill a glass with water and some watercolor paint. Can you see through the water? Yes, but not as well because the colored water is **translucent**. Only some light passes through.	Translucent means you can see through it a little, enough to see shapes but no detail.	The view from a window on a foggy day
Put only paint in the third glass. Paint is **opaque** and absorbs, or soaks up, most of the light and reflects the rest.	Opaque means you can't see through it.	The view from a window on a dark night

Middle School

During a study of ecosystems, using a text selection from *Sciencesaurus* to introduce the concept, have students download pictures that represent the parts of an ecosystem in their **Triple-Entry Vocabulary Journals**.

Word in Context	Your Definition	Your Memory Aid
A **species** is a group of organisms that can mate and produce offspring that, in turn, can produce more offspring.	Species are populations like humans or animals that have babies.	
All of the organisms of the same species that live in the same place at the same time make up a **population**.	A population is the whole group of the same type of species, like all of the deer in a forest.	A herd of deer
Populations do not live alone. They share the environment with other populations to form a **community**.	A community is a group of several populations, like all of the animals in the forest.	A variety of animals; birds in forest

High School

Inform students that they are to keep a daily technical vocabulary log called a **Triple-Entry Vocabulary Journal**. Let them work together during the first week as they study engineering careers, then expect them to continue on their own.

Word in Context	Your Definition	Your Memory Aid
Technologists work with existing technology to produce goods for society, like machines and equipment.	Technologists produce goods using technology that already exists.	Installation of office equipment in a new company to meet its needs
Engineers also apply technology for the betterment of society, but the engineer creates new technology through research, design, and development.	Engineers research and develop new technology and inventions.	Typewriter to computer • Film to digital camera • Maps to GPS systems

Social Studies

Elementary School

While reading a biography of Harriet Tubman, students create a **Triple-Entry Vocabulary Journal** and find pictures that fit each vocabulary word.

Word in Context	Your Definition	Your Memory Aid
Harriet's masters made her do housekeeping **chores**, but no one showed her what to do.	Work that has to be done around a house, like sweeping or washing dishes	Washing dishes at sink
They traveled by night and hid during the day, sometimes under the noses of people trying to catch them. Harriet used **disguises** and other tricks.	A costume or something that makes someone look different than they usually do	Halloween mask

Middle School

When reading the Preamble to the Constitution, keep a **Triple-Entry Vocabulary Journal** of the key concepts.

Word in Context	Your Definition	Your Memory Aid
After the Shay's Rebellion uprising, the writers of the Constitution realized that the national government must have the power to ensure **domestic tranquility**.	Peace and calm in the United States	
In order to form a **more perfect union**, the restatement of the concept of *E pluribus unum* (out of many, one), which many felt was important to get the states to work together.	Establishing a national government with federal powers could stop independent states from quarreling, thus creating a more perfect union.	A C B becomes ABC

High School

In a high school economics class, students better understand entrepreneurship by keeping a **Triple-Entry Vocabulary Journal** of technical vocabulary.

Word in Context	Your Definition	Your Memory Aid
Dry cleaners, appliance repair shops, and other small firms that provide very modest returns to their owners are called **marginal firms**.	A marginal firm has a limited ability to produce significant profits past compensation for time.	
Attractive small firms offer substantial rewards to the owner, earning $100,000 to $300,000 or more annually.	A small company that earns $100–300K after its costs is called an attractive small firm	$100,000 to $300,000 profit
A few businesses have such potential for growth that they are called **high-potential ventures** or **gazelles**.	Companies that grow at blinding speed, which make their founders rich when they go public	Facebook and YouTube

English Language Arts

Elementary School

During reading of Sewell's *Black Beauty,* students learn new vocabulary using context clues.

Word in Context	Your Definition	Your Memory Aid
I love horses and it **riles** me to see them badly used.	Upsets and angers	
Cruelty was the devil's own **trademark** and if we saw any one who took pleasure in cruelty we might know who he belonged to, for the devil was a murderer from the beginning.	A mark or picture that shows what someone is like	
Well, angry as I was, I was almost frightened. He roared and **bellowed** in such a style.	Make a loud scary noise	**BOOO!**

Middle School

To help students use key vocabulary terms from their reading when writing summaries of short stories (for example, London's *To Build a Fire*).

Word in Context	Your Definition	Your Memory Aid
His flesh was burning . . . The sensation developed into pain that grew **acute**.	Intense and strong	A sunburn can cause acute pain.
He disrupted the **nucleus** of the little fire, the burning grasses and tiny twigs separating and scattering.	The center of something that holds it together	Our grandmother was the nucleus of our family.

High School

When reading Hemingway's *The Old Man and the Sea,* use a **Triple-Entry Vocabulary Journal** to help students expand their knowledge of precise words.

Word in Context	Your Definition	Your Memory Aid
The dark cloud of blood had settled and **dispersed** in the mile deep sea.	To break apart; dispel	The group dispersed when bees came out of the hive.
The old man's head was clear and good now and he was full of **resolution**, but he had little hope.	Determination that a future action will be done	New Year's Resolution HAPPY NEW YEAR

Word Sort

Description

Word Sort is a classification strategy in which students cluster words in meaningful categories to discover main ideas or determine conceptual relationships (Gillet & Kita, 1979).

Common Core Connection	Instructional Shift
Word Sort can be a very simple strategy, or a very challenging one, depending on the words selected and the complexity of relationships.	1

Purpose

Use *before* and *after* reading to

- Help students learn vocabulary by comparing, contrasting, and classifying words based on characteristics or meanings.

- Help students recognize the relationships and differences between terms that are related to the same concept.

- Develop students' ability to reason through analysis, classification, induction, and analogy.

- Enhance students' interest in vocabulary development through a multisensory experience as they read, write, and manipulate words while sharing their thinking with others.

- Develop divergent thinking when open sort is used.

Directions

1. Have students copy terms to be sorted onto index cards, one word per card.

2. Direct students to sort the words into categories, either by providing the categories (closed sort) or having students generate the categories (open sort).

3. Ask students to share the reasoning and evidence for the way the vocabulary is sorted.

Example

Topic: Geometry—Solids, Circles, and Transformations

Words to Sort		
Pyramids	Radius	Translation
Prism	Diameter	Lines of symmetry
Reflection	Surface area	Isometric drawing
Circumference	Volume	Cone
Rotation	pi	Rotational symmetry
Categories		
Polyhedrons	Circles/Cylinders	Transformations

Source: Weizer (2003). Used with permission.

Extensions

Have students sort the words into a **Venn diagram**, then summarize their findings in a **Quick Write**.

Differentiation suggestion: Match the complexity of the vocabulary terms used in the sorts to students' varied instructional levels.

Word Sort Template

Name: _____

Date: _____

Categories		
Words to Sort		

© 2011 Public Consulting Group

Word Sort Content Examples

Mathematics

Open **Word Sort** (students determine the categories after discussing the words and sorting them into affiliate clusters).

Topic: Geometry and Measurement—Solid Figures and Processes of Measurement

Words to Sort		
Prisms	Base	Lateral faces
Platonic solids	Cone	Cylinder
Sphere	Pyramid	Polygons
Circumference	pi	Surface area
Volume	Cubic unit	Vertex

Science

Open **Word Sort** (students determine the categories after discussing the words and sorting them into affiliate clusters).

Topic: Erosion and Weathering

Words to Sort		
Aquifer	Glacier	Esker
Leaching	Terracing	Channel
Abrasion	Climate	Oxidation
Soil	Striation	Outwash

Social Studies

Closed **Word Sort** (teacher determines the categories for students to sort under).

Topic: Early American History

Categories		
People	Places	Common Concepts
Words to Sort		
Jamestown	Quakers	Pilgrims
Colony	Puritans	Indentured servitude
Slaves	Plymouth	Haven
Epidemic	Imports/exports	Pennsylvania

English Language Arts

Closed **Word Sort** (teacher determines the categories for students to sort under).

Topic: *Anne Frank: The Diary of a Young* Girl by Anne Frank

Categories		
Mood	Illness	Personality Trait
Words to Sort		
Melancholy	Poignant	Diphtheria
Despondent	Hypochondria	Superficial
Pensive	Dejected	Jocular
Malaria	Fanatic	Fatalistic

Developed by Roz Weizer. Used with permission.

Word Analysis

Description

Word Analysis is a way of analyzing the structure of unknown words to derive their meanings. Students deconstruct words into prefixes, roots, and suffixes and make connections between these and other words sharing similar parts. Readers often combine this strategy with the contextual analysis of the sentence or passage in which the word is found.

Common Core Connection	Instructional Shift
Word Analysis addresses CCRA.L.4 by supporting students in "analyzing meaningful word parts."	1

Purpose

Use *before* or *during* reading to

- Define unknown words.
- Make words memorable through understanding the parts that make up the word.
- Connect new vocabulary to words already known.
- Improve reading fluency.
- Improve reading comprehension.

Directions

1. Identify words in an upcoming reading selection that can be analyzed using their roots and affixes (prefix or suffix).

2. Focus instruction on identifying the root word and seeing how the prefix and suffix function together with the root to create the meaning of the word. Model this for the class.

3. Have students practice covering the prefixes and suffixes to see the root words, then follow with practice in adding and removing prefixes and suffixes and discussing how this changes the meaning of the word. Do this as a class and then direct students to continue in pairs or small groups, writing the meaning in the appropriate column on the template. Then review the definitions and see how close the student definitions were, making sure students correct and refine definitions as necessary.

4. Once students are comfortable with **Word Analysis**, teach them the specific root words that relate to the content area and topic(s) of learning by providing practice with many words with the same root and/or affix. Ask students to generate other words that use the same root or affix, divide the list into groups of words, and have pairs or small groups analyze how each group of words is similar

or different. This process of comparing words not only helps students more than memorizing a definition would, but it also contributes to an understanding of how word parts influence word meaning and reinforces words related to the same concept.

Extensions

Combine the study of word parts with instruction in the use of context clues.

Use vocabulary instruction strategies as appropriate to the specific words: **Word Analysis** for compound words like *piecemeal* or *uncomfortable* and *discomfort*, a **Concept Definition Map** or **Frayer Model** for more complex concepts like *freedom* or *power,* and a **Triple-Entry Vocabulary Journal** or **Interactive Word Wall** for technical terms that pertain to a specific topic like *algebra* or *electricity*.

Word Analysis Template

Name: _____

Date: _____

Content Unit/Topic_____

Directions

Write the unknown vocabulary words in the left column. Divide the word into its parts and then develop a possible definition for the word.

Word	Prefix	Root	Suffix	Definition

Word Analysis—Frequent Affixes and Roots

Prefixes		Suffixes	
a-, an-	mono-	-able, -ible	-ion, -tion, -ation, -ition
anti-	non-	-al, -ial	-ity, -ty
bi-	out-	-ed	-ive, -ative, -itive
co-	over-	-en	-less
counter-	pre-	-er, ier	-ly
de-	pro-	-er, -or	-ment
dis-	re-	-est	-ness
en-, em-	semi-	-ful	-ous, -eous, -ious
ex-	sub-	-ic	-s, -es
fore-	super-	-ing	-y
in-, im-	syn-		
in-, im-, il-, ir-	tele-		
inter-	trans-		
mid-	un-		
mis-	under-		

Common Greek and Latin Roots in English

Root	Meaning	Origin
aud	hear	Latin
astro, aster	star	Greek
auto	self	Latin
bene	good	Latin
bio	life	Greek
chrono	time	Greek
dict	speak, tell	Latin
duc	lead, make	Latin
gen	give birth	Latin
geo	earth	Greek
graph	write	Greek
jur, jus	law	Latin
luc	light	Latin
man	hand	Latin
meter	measure	Greek
min	little, small	Latin
mit, mis	send	Latin
omni	all	Latin
ped	foot	Latin
phon	sound	Greek
photo	light	Greek
port	carry	Latin
qui	quiet	Latin

scrib, script	write	Latin
sens	feel	Latin
spect	see	Latin
struct	build, form	Latin
tele	far off	Greek
terr	earth	Latin
vac	empty	Latin
vid, vis	see	Latin

KWL Plus

Description

KWL is a reading/thinking strategy that uses a three- or four-column graphic organizer for students to list (1) what they **know (K)** about a topic, (2) what they **want (W)** to learn about a topic, and (3) what they **learned (L)** about a topic after instruction or reading. **KWL Plus** adds mapping and summarization to the original KWL strategy. This helps students restructure text and rewrite to process information (Carr & Ogle, 1987).

Common Core Connection	Instructional Shift
As we work toward Instructional Shift 2, Reading, Writing, and Speaking Grounded in Evidence from Text, Both Literary and Informational, we should be cautious about relying too much on students' prior knowledge before they dig into the words of the text. However, teachers report that surfacing prior knowledge is a powerful way to engage students and create curiosity about a topic. **KWL Plus**, used before, during, and after reading, can serve as a formative assessment practice. This strategy can also serve as the basis for discussion or debate.	2

Purpose

Use *before*, *during*, and *after* reading to

- Activate and/or assess prior knowledge.
- Provide a preview of vocabulary or concepts.
- Help students be aware of their learning progress.
- Check for misconceptions.
- Support flexible grouping for differentiated instruction.

Directions

1. After an initial discussion, short reading, or video to activate prior knowledge about the topic, distribute copies of a **KWL Plus** chart, formatted with four columns with the headings *What I Know, What I Want to Know, What I Learned, What I Still Wonder About*.

2. Provide students with the topic you want them to think about and ask them to fill in the **K** column, listing what they already know about the topic.

3. Ask students to think about what they would like to learn about the topic. Encourage them to think of at least one idea to write in the **W** column. Have students brainstorm where to find this information and list this in the chart. Note: You can change W to N—*What They Need to Know*.

4. Students read the selection(s) provided or assigned and fill in the **L** column of the chart, listing the things they learned from the reading.

5. Discuss the accuracy of students' prior knowledge. If they still have questions, ask them to add these to the **+** column, *What I Still Wonder About*. This column could be the starting point for further research on a topic.

6. Students then use the **KWL Plus** worksheet to construct a concept map that categorizes all of the information they have learned about the topic.

Extensions

Have students write a summary of the topic.

Ask students to complete a **Quick Write** that describes the learning process: What did you already know before reading? What did you want to learn about? How did you approach learning about it? What did you find out?

KWL Plus Template

Name: _____

Date: _____

Directions

1. List what you **know (K)** about a topic, what you **want (W)** to learn about a topic, what you **learned (L)** about a topic after reading about it, and what you still wonder (**+**) about.

2. Create a **Concept Map** of your understanding of the topic.

K What I *Know*	W What I *Want* to Know	L What I *Learned*	+ What I Still Wonder About

KWL Plus Content Examples

Mathematics

During an introduction to statistics, use **KWL Plus** to help students identify questions they'd like to answer about their class or school.

Topic: Measurement and Data

K	W	L·	+
• 12 inches = 1 foot • We use inches for smaller measurements and feet for larger ones. • Area describes the space inside a shape. • "Square inches" and "square feet" are used when describing areas.	• What is the area of my desk? • What is the area of my group's table?	• My desk measures 24" x 18" so the area is 432 square inches, or 3 square feet. • There are 6 desks at our group's table, so 6 x 432 = 2,592 square inches, or 18 square feet.	• How many square feet of carpeting would we need to cover the entire classroom? • Half of the classroom?

Science

Use **KWL Plus** to build students' capacity to think about science in terms of proposing questions, answering them, and thinking of new questions.

Topic: Killer Whales

K	W	L	+
• Live in oceans • Are vicious • Eat other whales • Are mammals	• What kind of fish do they eat? • How long do they live? • How do they breathe?	• Weigh 10,000 lbs. and get 30 ft. long • Eat squids, seals, and dolphins • Are carnivorous • Breathe through blow holes • Have echolocation • Found in oceans • Are warm-blooded • Have good vision under water	• Why do they attack people? • How fast can they swim?

Social Studies

Before and *during* the study of the formation of the United States Constitution, have students fill out the first two columns of the **KWL Plus** chart. As students interact with texts and primary source documents, talk as a class about what these things tell them about the questions they originally asked. Afterward, have students identify new questions they will explore individually. Use these questions as the basis for poster sessions on this aspect of American History.

Topic: United States Constitution

K	W	L	+
• It was written a long time ago. • It's why we have the kind of government we have.	• Who wrote the constitution? • How did they think of it? • Is Freedom of speech in the Constitution? • A group of 55 men sort of wrote it together.	• They got lots of the ideas from John Locke, a philosopher, and they took some ideas from England's government. • Freedom of speech is in the Bill of Rights. That is a collection of amendments that got added soon after the Constitution was written.	• Was it hard to agree on all of the different parts? • When people had different ideas, how did they decide what to do? • What are the other parts of the Bill of Rights?

English Language Arts

Before, during, and *after* reading informational text about animal intelligence, have students complete what they know and want to know about the topic. During reading, have students collect what they are learning in the **KWL Plus** template. As a class, identify the most pressing questions students still have and use that information as a basis for research.

Topic: Animal Intelligence

K	W	L	+
• Humans can think. • Evidence exists showing animals can think.	• Are humans smarter than animals? • How could you prove humans are smarter than animals?	• Animals have unique perspectives and intelligences that humans don't possess.	• It's difficult to compare human and animal intelligence because they possess very different and unique strengths and traits.
• Humans are thought to be smarter than animals.	• How is animal intelligence measured?	• In many cases, animals possess traits that make them better at certain tasks than humans (for example, recent research describes animals' competence at social and cognitive tasks that humans often struggle with—like mastering conversational etiquette).	

Quick Write

Description

Quick Write is a versatile strategy used to develop writing fluency, build the habit of reflection into a learning experience, and informally assess student thinking. The strategy asks learners to respond in 2–10 minutes to an open-ended question or prompt posed by the teacher *before, during,* or *after* reading.

Common Core Connection	Instructional Shift
Quick Writes are one of the most valuable tools in your Common Core toolkit. They can be used before, during, and after reading and can be targeted toward checking for growing understanding of specific reading standards. Use the words of the standards in your prompt! Frequent Quick Writes help students fulfill the "range of writing" targeted in CCRA.R.10.	2

Purpose

Use *before, during,* and *after* reading to

- Activate prior knowledge by preparing students for reading, writing, or a discussion.
- Help students make connections.
- Promote reflection about key content concepts.
- Encourage critical thinking.
- Organize ideas for better comprehension.
- Increase background knowledge when shared.
- Synthesize learning and demonstrate understanding of key concepts.
- Reinforce vocabulary.
- Provide a purpose for reading.
- Assess student knowledge on the topic prior to reading.

Directions

1. Explain that a **Quick Write** engages students in thinking about a content topic before, during, and after reading. Stress that in a Quick Write students respond to a question or prompt related to the text by writing an informal response more concerned with content than with form. Typically, a Quick Write is graded only for completion, not for quality or accuracy.

2. Select a topic related to the text being studied and explain the purpose for the **Quick Write**.

Examples:

- Summarize what was learned.
- Connect to background information or students' lives.
- Explain content concepts or vocabulary.
- Make predictions, inferences, and hypotheses.
- Pose a question that addresses a key point in the reading selection.

3. Inform students how long they will have to do the writing, typically 2–10 minutes.

4. Use the **Quick Write** as part of instruction, assessment, and discussion.

Extensions

Quick Writes can be assigned as part of students' learning logs or journals.

Quick Writes can be used to think about or brainstorm for a **Think-Pair-Share**.

Students can generate their own **Quick Write** questions and prompts.

Students can share their **Quick Write** responses in small groups and compare their answers.

Students can work in small groups to create a **Quick Write**, with each student offering one sentence in a round-robin fashion.

Quick Write Content Examples

Mathematics

- How do you divide something into pieces?
- How much is a million?
- Describe the differences between a factor and a multiple?
- If you flip a coin 10 times, how many times do you think it will come up "heads"? Why do you think so?
- What's a prime number?
- What do you know about Pascal's Triangle?
- What does it mean to "square" something? For example, what does x2 mean?

Science

- *Before* studying an earth science unit about weathering, erosion, and deposition, have students do a **Quick Write** in their science notebooks, responding to the following prompt: "Does the surface of the Earth change? How do you know? What evidence do you have?"
- *After* a lesson on erosion, have students do a **Quick Write** on how erosion changes the surface of the Earth.
- *Before* a study about the cross-disciplinary theme of systems, elicit student thinking and prior knowledge by having them respond to a **Quick Write** prompt: "Where have you heard the word *system* before? How would you explain what it means?"
- *Before* studying a science-in-society unit, elicit students' prior knowledge using the following **Quick Write** prompt: "There are many conversations going on right now about global climate change and how to deal with it. What do you think global climate change is? How is the global climate changing? How do you know?"

Social Studies

- We are going to study recent efforts to achieve a Middle East Peace Accord. Who are the key political figures you think are likely to influence this effort?
- Imagine that you lived 30,000 years ago during the Stone Age. How did you use natural resources to survive?

English Language Arts

Aligned to the CCSS for Reading:

- Determine a central idea or theme of a text and analyze its development; summarize the key supporting details and ideas. (CCRA.R.2)
- Choose a character, an event, or an idea and describe how it develops and interacts over the course of the text. (CCRA.R.3)
- Analyze how the choice of a specific word or phrase shapes meaning or tone. (CCRA.R.4)

Partner/Small Group Vocabulary Preview

Description

The **Partner/Small Group Vocabulary Preview** is a reading strategy in which students collaboratively discuss and define vocabulary before reading a selection so that text comprehension during reading is enhanced.

Common Core Connection	Instructional Shift
CCRA.L.4 requires students to define unfamiliar words using context clues, meaningful word parts, and reference materials. However, the intent is that these words will be defined as they are met in context. The **Partner/Small Group Vocabulary Preview** might be best used after a first read of the text so that students know the gist of the piece, rather than before reading.	1

Purpose

Use *before* reading to

- Build word knowledge prior to reading.
- Provide opportunities for collaborative analysis of new vocabulary, using contextual and structural clues in the text as well as prior knowledge.
- Help struggling readers learn how to define words from the text context.
- Provide an interactive way to preview content reading selections and stimulate interest in reading.

Directions

1. Create a list of vocabulary words that students will need to understand in order to comprehend the text.

2. Use a **Think-Aloud** to model what you want students to do. Analyze four or five words using structural analysis (prefixes, affixes, roots) and context clues.

3. Have students work with partners or small groups to locate the vocabulary words. As each one is found, the group analyzes the context in which the word is used.

4. Students discuss whether anyone in the group can define the vocabulary term in his or her own words. All students who know the word should share their ideas and agree on a common definition. Students take notes on the definitions.

5. If no one in the group can define a word, students access other classroom resources that might help them understand it, such as a dictionary or text glossary. The definition should then be stated in their own words.

6. Bring students together for a whole-class discussion of the vocabulary terms and discuss the various definitions. Students should check the definitions they wrote in their notes to be sure they are accurate and add new information from the class discussion.

Extensions

Have students do a **Quick Write** to summarize the concept that connects the vocabulary words together.

Have students record their definitions in a **Triple-Entry Vocabulary Journal** that includes an example or illustration of the application of the words to help recall.

Develop an **Interactive Word Wall** with the vocabulary terms and students' definitions.

Create a **Concept Definition Map** for the most difficult words.

Have students compare their definitions with dictionary definitions.

Partner/Small Group Vocabulary Preview Template

Name: _____

Date: _____

Reading Selection: _____ Pages ___ – ___

Directions

Preview the reading selection to find new vocabulary terms and try to figure out what they mean. Analyze each word to see if there are structural clues, such as a prefix, suffix, or root. Then locate context clues in the sentence or nearby sentences. Discuss the word to find out what anyone already knows about its meaning. You may also use resources like the text glossary or a dictionary. Then define the terms in your own words on this chart.

Vocabulary Term	Clues to Its Meaning

Definition in Your Own Words

Vocabulary Term	Clues to Its Meaning

Definition in Your Own Words

Vocabulary Term	Clues to Its Meaning

Definition in Your Own Words

Interactive Word Wall

Description

An **Interactive Word Wall** is a systematically organized collection of displayed words. Both students and teachers can suggest additions to Word Walls. Students are asked to interact with words on the Word Wall on an ongoing basis. In this way, the words become an integral part of students' reading, writing, and speaking vocabulary.

Common Core Connection	Instructional Shift
An **Interactive Word Wall** can be used to generate and discuss connections among complex concepts. Deepen understanding and make this an active learning strategy by having students move concepts around on the wall or floor and explain new connections.	1

Purpose

Use *before, during,* and *after* reading to

- Build vocabulary related to a particular instructional focus.

- Help students develop analytical skills like classification and deduction.

- Support students in their writing and other composing activities.

- Build sight word reading fluency.

- Provide a visual reference tool to help students remember important words related to a specific topic or focus.

Directions

1. Create a list for an **Interactive Word Wall** that will help students deepen their vocabulary and enhance reading comprehension.

    Examples of Word Wall lists:

    - Words connected to an upcoming unit of study

    - Words connected to specific instructional areas (for example, math order of operations, historical terms, literary devices)

    - Difficult words found in a textbook chapter

    - Words connected to a theme, book, or author

    - Related root words with different prefixes and affixes

2. Refer to the **Interactive Word Wall** throughout the unit of study about the content concept it relates to, ensuring that students are actively interacting with the words on the wall.

Examples of interactive activities:

- Sort the words into categories and label them (**list-group-label** or **Word Sort**).

- Use three to five words on the wall to write a summary sentence about a main concept.

- Create an **Analytic Graphic Organizer** that relates the words to one another.

- Write a narrative piece—short story, poem, description—that links several words on the **Word Wall** together in a meaningful way.

- Create a word game using the words on the wall—a crossword puzzle, word search, paired compare/contrast.

Extensions

Have students keep a **Triple-Entry Vocabulary Journal** with terms on the **Interactive Word Wall**.

Have students create slide shows or visual presentations about the terms on the **Interactive Word Wall**.

Interactive Word Wall Planning Template

Name: _____

Date: _____

Directions

Think about the key ideas and concepts that will be covered in the text, other readings, or class instruction or discussion. Think of a way you could use an **Interactive Word Wall** to deepen students' understanding of vocabulary and course concepts. Define the learning purposes, some sample words, and three activities you could do to have students interact with the words.

Word Wall Concept _____

Learning Purpose _____

_____

Initial Word List (will be added to during unit)

_____   _____

_____   _____

_____   _____

_____

Interactive Activity 1

_____

_____

_____

_____

Interactive Activity 2

_____

_____

_____

_____

Interactive Activity 3

_____

_____

_____

_____

Interactive Word Wall Content Examples

English Language Arts

During and *after* reading and writing informative/explanatory essays

As students read exemplary informative/explanatory essays, create a **Word Wall** of transitional words and phrases, domain-specific vocabulary, and precise language to increase cohesion and clarity about a topic(s).

Have students interact with the words by

- Identifying transitional words during reading and discussing how they create cohesion and clarify the relationships among ideas and concepts in a text

- Identifying precise language and domain-specific vocabulary that informs or explains a topic(s)

- Revising a draft essay by adding transitional words and phrases or domain-specific vocabulary from the Word Wall

- Creating an original piece using at least 15 words or phrases from the Word Wall

- Editing one another's essay drafts to provide feedback about how specific word choices can improve clarity, cohesion, and precision

Mathematics

Before reading a text chapter on probability and solving problems related to coin and die tossing

Have students quickly peruse the chapter to identify what they think will be key terms related to probability—for example, *variable, distribution, reference class, set of possible values, experiment, outcome, event, sample space, probability of an event.*

Have students create their own **Triple-Entry Vocabulary Journal** entries about each word on the wall that include a definition in their own words and a visual memory aid.

Have students interact with **Word Wall** terms by

- Arranging and rearranging the words to demonstrate the conceptual connections between the words

- Adding terms to the Word Wall that amplify or clarify the terms

- Writing a short persuasive essay on the importance of understanding mathematical probability related to three or more Word Wall terms

Science

Before, during, and *after* reading articles in a computer technology course about the power of Internet connectivity

As the class reads articles about the Internet, have students create a **Word Wall** with important Internet terminology such as *search engine, algorithms, HTML, URL, IP address, blog, malware, phishing,* and *spam.*

Social Studies

During and *after* reading a chapter on the ways production, distribution, and consumption differ in various countries in a economics class

As students read about these systems, have them create **Word Wall** cards and post them under one of the three categories on the wall: production, distribution, and consumption.

Have students interact with these words by

- Creating **Triple-Entry Vocabulary Journal** entries about each word on the wall that include a definition in their own words and a visual memory aid

- Writing a short **Quick Write** defining the Internet or the World Wide Web, using at least nine terms from the Word Wall

- Drawing a **Venn diagram** that compares the World Wide Web and the Internet using Word Wall terms

Have students interact with these words by

- Scrambling the words on the wall and asking students to list and group the words into the three systems of production, distribution, and consumption

- Having students select a country they have studied and pick one word from each of the three systems that best represents that country's systems of production, distribution, and consumption

- Having students select a word from the wall and do a short charade or role play, while other students guess the word

Ideas for Increasing Student Interaction with Word Walls

Now that you've identified the important content area vocabulary words for your upcoming unit and you've decided how you'll display them in the room, what's next? How can you get your students to engage with the words on the **Interactive Word Wall** in ways that don't take up all of your class time, provide students with multiple exposures to the vocabulary, and include approaches based on effective vocabulary instruction? The goal is to build a culture of using technical terms correctly (for the context), descriptively (to communicate), analytically (to diagnose and problem solve), and functionally (when they complete tasks). The following are some ideas to get you started—you can probably think of many more!

When students are reading textbooks, manuals, articles, and similar resources.

- Provide points for finding or noticing **Word Wall** words in written material.
- Have students note where specific **Word Wall** words are found in print materials and add this information to the Word Wall. Students can compete in teams.
- Have students create definitions of **Word Wall** words as they read and then play matching games at the beginning of class for review or vote on the best definitions.
- Provide points if students suggest additional words for the **Word Wall** and can make a case for why the words are important to the unit of study.
- Have students mark present and past **Word Wall** words (as well as unfamiliar terms they encounter) when reading by underlining, using sticky notes, highlighting, and similar strategies.

When students are writing work summaries, logs, descriptions of how to complete certain processes, or Quick Writes/checks for understanding.

- Require the use of **Word Wall** words (two or three) in work reports, summaries, and the like.
- Require that all **Word Wall** terms be spelled correctly (because they are on the wall).
- Have students use **Word Wall** words in **Quick Writes** (for example, write down your two favorite words from the Word Wall and say why you like them; select two words from the Word Wall and describe how they are connected; write down everything you know about _____; compare and contrast two terms).

When students are talking about or presenting on a topic or demonstrating how to do something.

- Expect that **Word Wall** words be used to complete the assignment. Require that presentations use a certain number correctly.
- Have students "catch" other students using correct terminology.
- Post **Word Walls** in the classroom.
- Give points when students use **Word Wall** terms correctly when presenting or demonstrating.
- Make connections between **Word Wall** words and the topic at hand.
- Ask students to give synonyms, antonyms, examples, and nonexamples when they use a word from the **Word Wall**.

Simple games students can play to learn the technical terms.

- Play games with the **Word Wall** words such as *slap* (provide a definition and the first one to slap the definition with a flyswatter wins).

- Play *Jeopardy!* (What is . . . ?), "I'm thinking of," or charades with **Word Wall** words.

When students are discussing a topic in class, first learning about a topic, or reviewing the unit for a test.

- Have students complete a **Knowledge Rating Guide** with the words. Ask students to list the words under the appropriate heading: words they know and can explain, words they have heard of but are unsure what they mean, and words they have never heard of. Then discuss the words as a class.

- Ask students to list words from the **Word Wall** in a **Triple-Entry Vocabulary Journal** (word in context = first column; definition in own words = second column; picture or way to remember the meaning of the word = third column).

- Develop quadrant cards or **Frayer Models** for key concepts where students write the word in the center and give the definition, an example, a nonexample, and a picture of the word.

- Have students do **Word Sorts** in pairs where students work together to put **Word Wall** words into categories.

- Have students complete a **Concept Map** or **Semantic Feature Analysis** using the **Word Wall** words as they complete the unit.

Caution!

For most students . . .

Writing a word and its definition is not an effective way to learn vocabulary. Students tend to write down the first or shortest definition. To truly "own" a word, students need multiple repetitions in multiple contexts and to actively process the word (using a **Knowledge Rating Guide**, writing how two terms are connected, drawing a picture, giving examples and nonexamples, etc.).

For many students . . .

Flashcards can be effective for review but not as a way to "learn" words. Have students interact with the **Word Wall** words in many ways before using flashcards.

For all students . . .

A glossary list or definitions sheet is not a Word Wall. Word Walls are public displays of words designed to support all students' reading, writing, and learning about a topic. Students can (and should!) make their own personal vocabulary lists, flashcard stacks, or **Triple-Entry Vocabulary Journals**, but that should be in addition to the Word Wall.

Chapter Preview/Tour

Description

A **Chapter Preview/Tour** is a guided tour of the chapter about to be read that asks students to answer brief questions and make predictions related to chapter headings, vocabulary, text structure, and graphics.

Common Core Connection	Instructional Shift
Use the **Chapter Preview/Tour** to introduce informational text structures, but not as a regular practice. It should serve as a model for students and be considered Step 1 in a gradual release of responsibility. Ask students to revisit their previews after close reading to answer their questions and confirm their predictions. Also follow with a **Quick Write** to ask them how the parts of the text related to one another and the whole (CCRA.R.5).	3

Purpose

Use *before* reading to

- Provide an introduction to the text that will be read.
- Help students make connections by linking text information with their own knowledge.
- Identify how the text structure signals ideas and concepts.
- Draw students' attention to text features.
- Help students learn to use reading aids provided within the text.

Directions

1. Model how to complete the **Chapter/Preview Tour** template.
2. Initially give students guidance in what to look for—for example, bold vocabulary words, main ideas, broad concepts, text structure, important details, writing style, tone or mood, and themes.
3. Let students work collaboratively to preview text, complete a template, and share their ideas back to the whole class.
4. Have students complete the **Chapter/Preview Tour** independently.

Extensions

Have students describe in writing how the use of various text features helped them construct meaning from the text.

Modify the **Chapter/Preview Tour** template and ask students to work with you to collaboratively revise the template to match different types of text (journal article, website text, chapter in a novel).

Chapter Preview/Tour Template

Name: _____

Date: _____

Directions

As you look through the assigned chapter, respond to the following prompts.

Textbook

_____

Reading Assignment Chapter _____ Pages _____

1. What is the title of the chapter?

_____

Create a question from the title.

_____

2. List two headings or subheadings. Write a question for each.

Heading _____

Question _____

Heading _____

Question _____

3. Based on the *Introduction,* what will the chapter be about?

_____

_____

Based on the *Summary,* list two important ideas in the chapter.

a. _____

b. _____

Chapter Preview/Tour Template (continued)

Textbook

_____

4. List two important vocabulary words.

    a. _____

    b. _____

    How do they appear in the text?

_____

_____

5. What kind of information do you get from words, phrases, or sentences in special type?

_____

_____

    List two important terms or ideas pointed out in special type.

    a. _____

    b. _____

6. What types of visuals do they have in the chapter (charts, graphs, pictures, maps, etc.)?

_____

    List two important facts you learn from these visuals.

    a. _____

    b. _____

7. Based on your review, list the facts you already know about the topic of this chapter.

Developed by Roz Weizer. Used with permission.

Chapter Preview Content Examples

English Language Arts

Before and *after* reading a textbook section about magical realism

Build background knowledge about magical realism by reading a short excerpt from *100 Years of Solitude* and *The Bluest Eye*. Give students a **Chapter Preview** template modified for fiction.

Model how to fill out the template and have students complete the template in partners before reading the section.

After students have read, review the information gathered as a class and discuss which information pertains to the two excerpts students listened to at the beginning of the lesson.

Mathematics

Before reading a textbook section unit on factors and multiples

Provide an introduction to the unit by identifying the "big ideas," which include determining factors; generating multiples; and determining factorizations, including prime factorization of whole numbers.

Connect this to prior student learning about skip counting, multiplication and division facts, and testing divisibility rules.

Have students work in pairs to preview the unit and complete the modified template. Have each group share with the whole class their findings and one fact they already know about factors and multiples.

Science

Before reading an article or website about a topic

Explicitly teach students to navigate the resource, noticing and becoming acquainted with standard text features such as sidebars with factual notes, captions, labels, tables of contents, and indexes.

Modify the **Chapter Preview** template for each new text type and create prompts about concepts from your current science unit that challenge students to stop, think, and record specific ideas or questions related to what they are studying.

Social Studies

Before reading a chapter on the westward expansion

Have students work in groups of three to complete a **Chapter Preview** and then identify questions they have about the westward movement and American West in the 1800s.

List the questions and then have the groups read through the chapter and also review several websites such as www.pbs.org/weta/thewest/ to find answers to the lists of questions generated by the groups.

Then complete a class **KWL Plus** chart that indicates what the class now knows and wants to learn in preparation for selection of individual research projects on the topic.

Anticipation/Reaction Guide

Description

An **Anticipation/Reaction Guide** is a questioning strategy that assesses prior knowledge and assumptions at the prereading stage and evaluates the acquisition of concepts and use of supporting evidence after reading (Duffelmeyer & Baum, 1992; Herber, 1978).

Common Core Connection	Instructional Shift
An **Anticipation/Reaction Guide** reinforces the importance of using evidence to support claims in reading, writing, and speaking.	2

Purpose

Use *before, during,* and *after* reading to

- Forecast and cue major concepts in the text to be read.

- Motivate students to want to read text to see if prior knowledge is confirmed or disproved.

- Require students to make predictions.

- Activate students' existing background knowledge and set a purpose for reading text.

- Focus readers on the main ideas presented in text.

- Help readers assess for misconceptions and reader–text discrepancies.

- Create active interaction between reader and text.

- Provide pre- and post-assessment information.

Directions

1. Identify the important ideas and concepts students should focus on when reading.

2. Create four to six statements that support or challenge students' beliefs, experiences, and preexisting ideas about the topic. The statement should be reasonably answered either way.

3. Set up a table for student responses using the template.

Example of Anticipation Reaction Guide *before* and *after* Reading an Article on Healthy Food

BEFORE READING				AFTER READING	
Agree	Disagree	Statement	Page(s) Where Evidence Found	Agree	Disagree
		Diet soda is better for you than soft drinks with sugar.			
		Pasta is healthy for you.			
		Chocolate is bad for your teeth.			

4. *Before* reading the text, have students react to each statement in the *Before Reading* column individually and be prepared to support their positions.

5. In small groups or as a whole-class discussion, ask students to explain their initial responses to each statement.

6. Ask students to read the selection to find evidence that supports or rejects each statement.

7. *After* reading the text, ask students to react to each statement in the *After Reading* column to determine if they have changed their minds about any of the statements.

Extensions

Have students use additional sources of information to support opinions.

Ask students to rewrite any false statements based on the reading, individually or in cooperative groups.

Anticipation/Reaction Guide Template

Name: _____

Date: _____

BEFORE READING		Statement	Page(s) Where Evidence Found	AFTER READING	
Agree	**Disagree**			**Agree**	**Disagree**
Conclusion(s)					

Anticipation/Reaction Guide Content Examples

English Language Arts *Before, during,* and *after* reading *Romeo and Juliet* Have students anticipate and react to the text, using the response headings of *Agree/Disagree,* including statements such as: • Romeo is a foolish character. • *Romeo and Juliet* can be read as a comedy. • The events that take place in *Romeo and Juliet* could happen today.	**Mathematics** *Before, during,* and *after* reading a math textbook chapter on percents Have students anticipate and react to the text, using the response headings of *True/False,* including statements such as: • A 20% off sale is better than a buy-one-get-one free sale. • A mortgage of $1,000 at 5% for 30 years is more expensive to pay off than $1,000 at 7% for 30 years.
Science *Before, during,* and *after* reading a global warming report issued by international scientists Have students anticipate and react to the text, using the response headings of *Supported by Evidence/Not Supported by Evidence,* including statements such as: • Increasingly hotter temperatures around the globe show global warming is occurring. • Hurricanes will continue to increase in frequency, especially in southern locations. • Human causes are the leading reason for global warming.	**Social Studies** *Before, during,* and *after* reading an informational website on voting Have students anticipate and react to the text, using the response headings of *Accurate/Misrepresentation,* including statements such as: • More people voted for Independents in 2012 than in 2008. • Fewer people identified as Democrat or Republican in the 2012 election than ever before.

108   **Thinkquiry Toolkit 1** • Part 3

Use of *Triple-Entry Vocabulary Journal* in a High School Science Classroom

Ms. Pritchett knew her students were experiencing difficulty understanding the vocabulary of the biology text. She tried asking students to maintain a vocabulary notebook with the glossary definitions of the biology terms, but they were not successful on tests and could not seem to explain some of the science processes they had studied. How could she better help students connect vocabulary with understanding of science concepts? She knew it must move beyond memorization and writing of definitions. She decided to use the **Triple-Entry Vocabulary Journal** because it would give students the opportunity to develop a personal definition based on their understanding of the word used in context, along with representative diagrams and connections to each term.

Before Reading/Learning

Ms. Pritchett began the class by taking a large mass of dough and slowly stretching it apart at the center until it formed two new balls of dough. She asked students, "What just happened?"

Josh raised his hand. "You just made two balls out of one?"

"Today, we will begin a biology process that does something similar. We will learn about a process called *mitosis* and begin to understand the phases of mitosis by exploring the meaning of the terms or vocabulary. Before we look at the vocabulary, let's take a look at a brief animation of *Animal Cell Mitosis*." Afterward, Ms. Pritchett asked Martin what he observed during the animation.

Martin shrugged and said, "I saw a bunch of squiggly things moving apart and dividing."

Ms. Pritchett said, "Exactly," and wrote his observation on the interactive whiteboard.

"Now, let's carry this further by breaking it down into sequences or phases. What did you see happening at the beginning of the animation?"

Billy volunteered an observation: "There was a single object that began to stretch apart."

"Great! Did you see any similarity to the ball of dough?" Several students nodded their heads. Ms. Pritchett wrote Billy's observation on the interactive whiteboard. "What else did you notice?"

Mary said, "It looked as though the further the ball stretched, the thinner it got in the center." Ms. Pritchett jotted the observation down.

Johnson said, "When it stretched really far, the ball actually divided and formed two new balls that looked exactly the same, just smaller." Ms. Pritchett recorded the last observation.

Ms. Pritchett said, "Before we begin our study of mitosis, we need to work with the vocabulary so that you can understand what you will be reading and learning about this topic." She handed out a template for the Triple-Entry Vocabulary Journal, which had three columns labeled *Word in Context, Definition in My Own Words,* and *Picture, Memory Aid, or Phrase*. "We will be using this journal format today to help you as you record and learn new vocabulary related to cell division. Let's start with the word *mitosis*."

"Turn in your book to the section on mitosis. Listen as I read the definition aloud: *Mitosis is the process in which a cell duplicates its chromosomes to generate two identical cells.* Hmmm," Ms. Pritchett said as she thought aloud. "I think *duplicate* means making a copy of something, like making a copy of a picture on a copier. So I know mitosis has something to do with making copies of chromosomes before it actually generates, or makes, two new cells." Using the interactive whiteboard, Ms. Pritchett modeled how to write the use of the word in context by including the phrase in which it is found and the page number. "But, I want a simpler definition I can understand. What do you think about this one? *Mitosis happens when a cell divides perfectly to form two new cells that are exactly alike.*" Several students nodded.

Scott said, "Yeah, that sounds right." She wrote her own definition in the middle column, *Definition in My Own Words.*

"Okay, in the last column, I want to give an example or put in a visual that will help me remember the meaning of the word. For *mitosis,* I am going to connect it with the bread dough, which I divided into two identical balls. You can draw a picture, use clip art, include an example, or draw a diagram— whatever you think will help you to remember the definition."

"Before you begin working with a partner, I'd like you to look at the words connected with the phases of mitosis." She projected a **Word Splash** visual using **WordArt** of six vocabulary words: *interphase, prophase, metaphase, anaphase, telophase,* and *cytokinesis.* She pronounced each of the words and then asked students to scan the text to locate the words. She reminded students to record the page numbers next to the words so that they could easily return to the words in the text as they worked to complete the vocabulary study.

During Reading/Learning

Ms. Pritchett knew the vocabulary might serve as a stumbling block for many students, so she decided to read the initial section of the text aloud, pausing to let students reread sentences that included one of the vocabulary words. She also provided time for students to think and talk about the word and make any notes or ask questions.

When she finished reading the introductory section aloud, Ms. Pritchett wanted to be sure that each student understood how to use the Triple-Entry Vocabulary Journal before working with a partner on the rest of the mitosis vocabulary. The class worked with the first two words as a large group. She asked each student to individually record the context meaning of *interphase* and write the meaning in his or her own words. She asked one or two students to share their personal definitions. Ms. Pritchett said, "I'm not looking for a Rembrandt. I only want the diagram to have meaning to you so that you can remember the word." She guided the students as a class to complete the same process with *prophase.*

Ms. Pritchett continued the lesson by asking students to work with a partner to read over the text together once more. She suggested looking for context clues in the surrounding sentences, captions, charts, and diagrams.

"But what if there isn't a clue?" asked Allie.

"If you do not feel as though you have enough information, turn to the glossary to read a complete definition. Once you feel confident that you understand the meaning of the word, close the book and discuss your definition with your partner before writing your own definition in column two. Then, in column three, draw a diagram of the phase of mitosis or write some personal connection with the phase. The goal is to create an aid to help jog your memory so that you will clearly understand and remember the meaning of the word."

Ms. Pritchett circulated the room to provide assistance as needed. She reminded several students to be precise when paraphrasing the text definitions. She noticed that two students seemed to be struggling with how to complete the assignment, so she provided more explicit instruction on how to find the words and write their own definitions.

To help students develop a deeper understanding of the phases of mitosis, Ms. Pritchett had set up different stations in the lab using the microscopes and prepared slides to demonstrate the different phases of mitosis. The stations were purposely randomly arranged and not labeled as to the phases of mitosis. She asked students to move as groups of four to view the slides and to identify the correct labels and order for the six phases. She asked them to add information they observed in the third column of their Triple-Entry Vocabulary Journals if it added to their understanding of that particular phase.

After Reading/Learning

To determine the level of student understanding, Ms. Pritchett asked students to complete a **Quick Write** to explain the sequence of divisions, or phases, the cell moves through to form two daughter cells from one parent cell. She gave students a moment to reflect on and think about the vocabulary, animation, and slides they had worked with during class and encouraged them to use the information from their Triple-Entry Vocabulary Journals. She stressed that the purpose of the Quick Write is not to test them but to give them another way to practice using the vocabulary and to think about the concept of mitosis. It was encouraging to see that almost all of the students were writing, as this was not always the case. She knew that some students would need additional support to use the Triple-Entry Vocabulary Journal, but she felt that students' engagement during today's lesson indicated a positive connection with the strategy and learning new vocabulary. She resolved to ask students if they found the strategy helpful when class met the next day.

PART 4: Building New Knowledge *during* Reading/ Learning

Introduction

In the classroom, we often ask students to read, learn, and communicate their learning in some way. But, when students are assigned reading without being required to engage with the text in a concrete way during reading, they are less likely to comprehend and remember what they read.

The tools in this section of the Toolkit, Building New Knowledge, were selected to help students develop the habits and skills of engaging and making meaning of text. Many of the tools relate to note taking and organizing content for future use. These are skills that many students need help to develop. You will find a selection of student learning strategies and collaborative routines designed to help students interact with vocabulary and text during reading and learning. Many of these tools can also be used to support writing and discussion activities after reading and learning.

In this section of the Toolkit, you will find the following approaches to supporting reading and learning:

	Reading and Learning Phases		
	Before	During	After
Student Learning Strategies			
Analytic Graphic Organizers		✓	✓
Semantic Feature Analysis (all content areas)	✓	✓	✓
Discussion Web (Social Studies)		✓	✓
Proposition/Support Outline (Science and Social Studies)	✓	✓	✓
Inference Notes Wheel (English Language Arts)		✓	✓
Question-Answer Relationship (QAR)		✓	
Coding/Comprehension Monitoring		✓	
Two-Column Note Taking		✓	✓
Question the Author (QtA)		✓	
Collaborative Routines			
Think-Pair-Share	✓	✓	✓
Reciprocal Teaching		✓	
Paired Reading		✓	
Classroom Scenario			
Use of *Coding/Comprehension Monitoring* in an Elementary Social Studies Classroom		✓	

Question-Answer Relationship (QAR)

Description

Question-Answer Relationship (QAR) teaches students to assess the thinking demands of a passage and develop answers for four types of questions: *Right There* (the answer is directly stated in text); *Think and Search* (the answer is in the text but not stated directly); *Author and Me* (the answer is not in the text but is derived from integrating the author's information with background knowledge and experiences); and *On My Own* (the answer is not in the text; the reader must develop the answer using outside sources) (adapted from Raphael, 1982, 1984).

Common Core Connection	Instructional Shift
Question-Answer Relationship (QAR) is a valuable tool for teaching students how to recognize different types of text-dependent questions. In the original version of this strategy, *On My Own* questions were likely to be opinion questions, loosely connected to the topic of the text. In the era of college and career standards, teachers and textbook authors are asking far fewer *On My Own* questions. The emphasis is on reading, writing, and speaking grounded in evidence from the text. If the student can answer without having read the text, it's not a text-dependent question! Consider reframing *On My Own* questions as launch pads from this text to other texts on the topic: "Hmm, the author doesn't answer that question. I'll need to research to find the answer."	2

Purpose

Use *during* reading to

- Characterize questions and know how to construct the answers using the text, where applicable.
- Become more analytical and evaluative about responding to questions.
- Separate factual, implied, inferred, and predictive information while reading.
- Determine the supporting evidence for responses to questions.

Directions

1. Prepare a sample text reading with several questions that correspond to the four **QAR** types.
2. Explain that this strategy helps readers determine how to seek answers for questions about the text.
3. Show students the four types of **QAR** questions.

Right There	Think and Search
The answer is stated directly in the text.	The answer is in the text but not stated directly. The reader interprets the meaning from different parts of the text.
Author and Me	**On My Own**
The answer is not in the text. The reader must read the text in order to answer but must use personal knowledge with the information provided by the author.	The answer is not in the text. The reader must develop the answer based on knowledge and personal experience only.

4. Introduce several examples of *Right There* questions, then introduce several *Think and Search* questions. Emphasize that both types of questions require locating information within the text.

5. Introduce several *Author and Me* and *On My Own* questions for the same text reading.

6. Provide guided practice in small groups with several progressively longer pieces of text.

7. As students become more proficient, provide independent practice and give feedback to individual students about their **QAR** choices.

8. Once students can effectively use **QAR** to answer questions, have them generate their own questions to practice the various types and use QAR independently.

Extension

Link the **QAR** types of questions to **Critical Thinking Cue Questions**: *Right There* to knowledge; *Think and Search* to comprehension and application; *Author and Me* to analysis; and *On My Own* to evaluation and synthesis.

Question-Answer Relationship (QAR) Content Examples

Mathematics

Elementary School

Use **QAR** to help students determine if they need to use the glossary or go back to an earlier part of the chapter.

Example of teacher introduction of QAR, using guided questions:

Teacher: What is a fraction?

Student: It says it is a name for part of a whole.

Teacher: Yes, the answer is in the book. It's a *Right There* question. But what about this statement: *You name fractions by their numerators and denominators.* What do these words mean?

Student: It doesn't say.

Teacher: Look around the entire page. Can you see the definition anywhere?

Student: Yes, it's in a box on the next page.

Teacher: So sometimes you have to *Think and Search* to find an answer. That's another type of question, *Think and Search.* But what if the words weren't defined in that box?

Student: I'd have to look it up?

Teacher: Yes, you'd be on your own to learn it or you'd use hints from the book plus what you already know to figure it out. Sometimes you figure out and answer from the author and your own mind. That's called an *Author and Me* question. Or, if no answer is in the book, that's called an *On Your Own* question because you have to find the answer without help from the book.

Middle School

Use a **QAR** during a Mathscape lesson on nets that catch cubes to help students understand that they must read the text, analyze the graphics, and use their own knowledge to figure out the math. After explaining the four types of QAR questions, show them a completed QAR chart with both the question and the answer in the four quadrants.

Right There	**Think and Search**
What is a net?	What happens when I change the dimensions to the shape? How is it different for a two-dimensional shape versus a three-dimensional shape?
It says right in the text that it is "a 2-D figure that can be folded on its segments or curved on its boundaries to form a 3-D shape."	I have to use the computer application and the text to get the answer.
Author and Me	**On My Own**
What is a three-dimensional shape?	How many different nets can there be for a cube?
I know from the picture that it's like a box. I know from my own experience that a box has shape and isn't flat like it looks on the page. So I can guess that *dimension* means a shape that isn't flat.	Nothing in these pictures shows me the answer. The text doesn't tell me either. I'd have to draw it or look it up in another book.

High School

Before, during, and *after* reading a variety of data charts and graphs, use **QAR** to help students determine if the answer is provided in the data display or whether analysis, manipulation, computation, or calculation is needed to respond to the different kinds of questions.

Teacher-Generated Responses to Model QAR for Data Analysis

Right There	Think and Search
The specific number is provided.	The answer is there, but I need to understand the structure of the chart to locate the answer.
Author and Me	**On My Own**
I can figure out the answer from the data if I do some calculations.	The data doesn't provide a specific answer. I have to manipulate the data and figure it out on my own.

Science

Elementary School

When students are unsure how to do a science lab, help them understand when they must follow the lab directions or when they must think on their own by modifying the **QAR** cues they've already studied in reading.

Teacher-Modified Terms for QAR in Science

Right There	Think and Search
The directions tell me to do it.	I have to read the directions and also look at the illustrations.
Author and Me	**On My Own**
I have to follow the directions, but I also need to know what the words mean.	When the lab question says, *What do you think?*, it's a cue that I have to figure it out. The answer won't be in the book.

Middle School

While preparing students for a standardized test in science, help them understand the different kinds of questions that may be on the test and how to select the multiple-choice answer.

Teacher-Designed Cues for Using QAR Question Types to Analyze Test Questions

Right There	**Think and Search**
Does the question ask for just one fact? It's probably a *Right There* question.	Does the question ask you to choose several answers? It's probably a *Think and Search* question.
Author and Me	**On My Own**
Does the question ask about something the text doesn't fully explain? You will need to add your own knowledge to what the author has said.	Is the question a prompt that asks what you think? Then you have to form an opinion and support it with information from the passage.

High School

After reading a variety of articles on global warming, have students who already know **QAR** create their own questions. Provide a set of cue words to help them analyze the facts and opinions in the articles in their discussion groups.

Teacher-Created Cue Words to Guide Students in Generating QAR Questions

Right There	**Think and Search**
Who, where, list, when, how many, name, what, based on this passage	Summarize, what caused, contrast, explain, retell, how did, find
Author and Me	**On My Own**
In what instances?	Make a claim about global warming and support it with information from the passages you read.

Social Studies

Elementary School

During reading of a nonfiction book about Harriet Tubman, have students answer questions and write them in the **QAR** quadrant that they used to figure them out.

Teacher-Generated Questions

Right There	Think and Search
What made Harriet very unhappy when she was a child?	What were some ways in which Harriet showed courage?
Author and Me	**On My Own**
What caused Harriet's sleeping spells?	What is your opinion of Harriet's husband John, based on his interactions with Harriet?

Student Response to These Questions

Right There	Think and Search
It says on page 13 that she was hired out when she was just six years old and that many masters treated her badly.	She escaped a second time from slavery after her brothers forced her to return with them the first time. She repeatedly helped lead other slaves to freedom.
Author and Me	**On My Own**
Harriett was hurt by an iron weight. Weeks later she had sleeping spells. My mom wasn't sick at first with her cancer, but it made her sick later. So I think the iron weight caused the sleeping spells.	At first I liked him because he was a freeman who married a slave. But later he married someone else while Harriet was gone. When she came back to get him, he wanted her to stay. He was not a very honorable man.

Middle School

When students struggle with map interpretation, help them apply the **QAR** strategy they use in reading text to study of the map.

Teacher Application of QAR Types to Maps

Right There	Think and Search
The answer is on the map, such as a name of a city.	The answer is partly on the map, but you must use the map key to understand what the symbol or color means.
Author and Me	**On My Own**
The answer is on the map, but you have to understand what the vocabulary means to answer the question.	There is nothing on the map or in the map key that gives the answer. You'll need to use another source to find the answer.

High School

When students struggle to understand a complex world history textbook, check that they are using all of the information in charts, sidebars, chapter summaries, and illustrations to understand the content.

Teacher Explanation of Text Features

Right There	Think and Search
Look for an answer that is directly stated in words.	Put the answer together using the words, pictures, and charts
Author and Me	**On My Own**
Figure out the answer by combining what you already know with the information that is given.	Nothing in the words, pictures, or charts tells the specific answer. You must conduct a brief search to answer a question or solve a problem, demonstrating understanding of the subject under investigation.

English Language Arts

Elementary School

When reading "The Wolf in Sheep's Clothing" from Aesop's Fables, have students who have already used the **QAR** strategy several times develop their own QAR questions from the text.

Student Example of QAR Questions for "The Wolf in Sheep's Clothing"

Right There	Think and Search
Why does the wolf try to trick the shepherd?	What word would you use to describe the wolf in this fable?
Author and Me	**On My Own**
What moral is the author trying to communicate in this fable?	Contrast the moral of this fable with a new fable, "The Wolf and the Shepherd." How are the two stories similar? How are they different?

Middle School

After reading a selection that is followed by comprehension questions, use **QAR** to help students understand whether the questions are literal or require analytical, evaluative, or inferential thinking.

Teacher-Generated Questions to Model QAR for *Bud, Not Buddy*

Right There	Think and Search
What did Bud do to Todd?	Choose several examples of figurative language in the text and describe their impact on the story's tone.
Author and Me	**On My Own**
Why has the author used the word *gray* repeatedly here? What does the repeated use of the word *gray* emphasize to the reader?"	Write a literary argument essay in which you will establish a claim about whether Bud uses his "rules to live by" to help him survive or thrive in his life.

High School

Introduce the **QAR** strategy with a visual, such as *The Scream* by Edward Munch. Model the thinking behind the four types of questions by having students explain how they figured out the answer and then telling them the QAR type (Raphael, 1982).

Teacher: How many people are in this image?

Student: Three men. The men are right there in the image.

Teacher: This is a *Right There* question. The answer is right there for you to see.

Teacher: What is the setting in this image? How did you figure it out?

Student: It's during the day, on a bridge, near the ocean or a river. I looked at different parts of the image.

Teacher: This is a *Think and Search* question. It's in the image, but you have to look in several different places to figure out the entire answer.

Teacher: Is the man in the foreground the protagonist/hero or is he the antagonist/victim?

Student: He looks mean. I think he's the villain. I know a man who scowls like that and he's really mean. I used some clues from the image and what I already know to figure it out.

Teacher: This is an *Author and Me* question. You use information in the image and in your own head to answer the question.

Teacher: What is the overall impact of the image on you as a viewer?

Student: The image feels startling. We don't know from this image why the subject is screaming, but it seems likely that it was caused by fear, which is highlighted by the red fiery sky and the wavy blue water that seems to want to swallow the subject up.

Teacher: This is an *On My Own* question. You have to use both your personal reaction and the evidence in the image in order to answer the question on your own.

Coding/Comprehension Monitoring

Description

Coding/Comprehension Monitoring is a strategy that helps students to engage and interact with text and monitor comprehension as they read.

Common Core Connection	Instructional Shifts
Coding is an annotation shortcut that helps students focus on the purpose for close reading. On subsequent close readings, you may want students to use different codes.	1, 2, 3

Purpose

Use *during* reading to

- Support content area learning by focusing on key concepts.

- Provide a way for students to engage in a dialogue with the author.

- Help students identify how they process information while reading.

- Help students identify what is difficult in the text so that they can select and apply comprehension strategies to support their reading.

- Develop metacognitive awareness and ability to monitor one's own comprehension.

Directions

1. Explain that this strategy helps readers monitor their reading so that they can identify what they do or don't understand.

2. Choose two or three codes that support the purpose of the reading and reinforce targeted literacy habits and skills.

3. Model the strategy using an overhead or interactive whiteboard.

4. Guide students to apply the coding strategy. Review the codes and have students code their reactions, as they read, on the page margins, lined paper inserts, or sticky notes.

Possible Codes (use only two to four codes per time)

+	New information	!	Interesting
*	I know this information	—>	Important information
?	I don't understand/I have questions	T-T	Text-to-text connection
P	Problem	T-W	Text-to-world connection
S	Solution	T-S	Text-to-self connection
✓	I agree	C	Cause
X	I disagree	E	Effect

Extensions

Have students compare and discuss how they coded sections of the text.

After students are comfortable with coding using teacher-provided codes, encourage them to develop additional codes appropriate for reading a particular text.

Coding/Comprehension Monitoring Template

Name: _____

Date: _____

Note:

This template is useful if students cannot write in or mark the text directly and sticky notes are not available for use.

Page	Page	Page	Page	Page	Directions
					Insert this sheet in your book behind the reading assignment. As you read each page, write the page number at the top of the column. Then place the code directly across from the part of the text you are coding. Each time you read a new page, pull out this sheet to the corresponding next page and add your codes.
					Write down the two to four codes you will use to monitor your comprehension as you read the assignment.
					__ = _____
					__ = _____
					__ = _____
					__ = _____

Coding Content Examples

Mathematics

Elementary School

After reviewing addition, subtraction, multiplication, and division rules at the beginning of the school year, have students code a variety of written problems to find the cue words in the passage that tell them whether adding, subtracting, multiplying, or dividing is required to solve the problem.

Codes

A = Addition

S = Subtraction

M = Multiplication

D = Division

Middle School

Show students that coding of text is similar to coding of math problems. Explain that coding is a way to understand the patterns of written text, just like manipulatives are a physical code to help students see the patterns in mathematical problems. Model mathematical coding using the Lab Gear blocks in Mathscape's *Exploring the Unknown* lessons on writing and solving equations. Have them practice mathematical coding by using a set of blocks to illustrate a written expression, such as $x^2 + 5 + x = y^2$, followed by rearranging the blocks to combine like terms, $3x^2 + 2x + 5$.

Codes

Yellow blocks = Constants
Blue blocks = Variables

High School

While reviewing for the SATs, show students that coding is an effective way to remember how to compute the sine, cosine, and tangent of an angle. Remind them of the acronym SOHCAHTOA. Give a set of sample problems that require computing the sine, cosine, and tangent of an angle and have them code the problems using SOHCAHTOA.

Codes

SOH: Sine = Opposite/hypotenuse

CAH: Cosine = Adjacent/hypotenuse

TOA: Tangent = Opposite/adjacent

Science

Elementary School

During a lesson on the circulatory system, assess students' prior knowledge and current understanding by having them code in the margins of the handout.

Codes

! = I already know this information

? = I don't understand/I have questions

V = New vocabulary

X = I thought differently

Middle School

During a lesson on the reproduction of plants, introduce coding as a method to identify patterns and relationships in text the same way labels help you identify the patterns or relationships of a photograph or diagram. Using guided questioning, have students determine codes for an illustration of the life cycle of an apple: *pollination, fertilization, fruit development,* and *seed dispersal.*

Have students conduct online research in pairs to find articles about the reproduction of maples, lemons, peas, or tomatoes; print out the article and code the text for the stages of reproduction.

Codes

P = Pollination

F = Fertilization

D = Fruit development

S = Seed dispersal

High School

In a human anatomy and physiology class where coding has already been frequently used, have students skim and scan their independent reading handouts to identify key focus areas, define codes, and code the article in the margins. Use the coded assignments to confirm that assigned reading has been done and to monitor individual progress with text comprehension.

Directions to students: Skim the assigned reading. Determine the key types of information you will need to understand. Select two to four codes that will help you focus while you read. You may use any of the following codes or define your own codes.

Codes

V = New vocabulary

! = Key information to remember

F = Function

T = Important theory

M = Measurement or calculation

P = Procedure

A = Abnormality

S = Sequence or cycle

C = Cause

E = Effect

Social Studies

Elementary School

Introduce coding with map study before teaching students how to code text. Have students review the maps of three different states and mark the codes on the laminated maps with washable markers. Then have students read in the text about the states they chose using the following codes.

Codes

C = Capital city

H = Historical events happened here

P = Places of interest

W = Name of large bodies of water in or bordering a state

Middle School

While reading the text chapter on European explorers and the colonizing of North America, have students code both the text and the maps to identify which countries explored the different areas of North America.

Codes

P = Portugal

S = Spain

N = Netherlands

E = England

F = France

High School

When reading the Declaration of Independence, have students code the document in order to compare and make connections with the grievances of that time to today's world.

Codes

Y = Yes, this grievance is still important today.

N = No, this grievance is not as relevant today.

X = I don't see why this was a problem then or now.

? = I don't know if this grievance fits our society now.

English Language Arts

Elementary School

In a unit about champions, model for students how to code the attributes of a champion, using a short article or story about an Olympic champion. Provide several articles about different kinds of champions in life, such as firefighters or scientists, for them to read and code in pairs using the same codes. Ask the librarian to put together a group of stories and online articles about champions in diverse occupations. Have students select their own texts to practice coding independently, using the same codes to identify the attributes of a champion.

Codes

T = Talent

D = Dedication and determination

W = Hard work and practice

! = Passion to be the best

Middle School

During a poetry unit, help students understand the impact sound has on the reader by using coding to identify the techniques the poets use to achieve different sound effects. After teaching the elements of sound, have students work in pairs to code several poems. Reinforce student understanding of coding by having students independently practice coding with the same set of poems, using a second set of codes for figurative language.

Codes for sound

R = Rhyme

M = Meter

A = Alliteration and assonance

O = Onomatopoeia

Codes for figurative language

I = Imagery

P = Personification

S = Simile

M = Metaphor

High School

During a unit on analyzing essays, use coding to help students see how literacy devices and style conventions are used by authors to create interest or persuade readers to share their points of view. Using the topic of the environment, model coding with an excerpt from Rachel Carson's *Silent Spring*. Then have students work in small groups to analyze four environmental essays that vary in style, length, and reading difficulty such as Benjamin Franklin's *The Whistle*, Annie Dillard's *In the Jungle*, E. B. White's *Cold Weather*, Harry Crews' *The Hawk Is Flying*, Edward Abbey's *Desert Images*, R. J. Heathorn's *Learn with BOOK*, or a longer essay from John McPhee's *Control of Nature*. Have students share devices they coded and explain how they contributed to the reader's understanding of the author's point of view.

Codes

I = Information

D = Description

P = Persuasion

V = Voice and word choice

Two-Column Note Taking

Description

The **Two-Column Note Taking** strategy can be used with text, lectures, or when viewing media presentations to help students organize their thinking about specific content. It is sometimes called a *double-entry journal* when used with fictional text or when the focus is on a student's argumentative or informative/explanatory response to the text instead of on "taking notes." When combined with a summary, it may be referred to as "Cornell Notes" (Pauk, 1962).

Common Core Connection	Instructional Shifts
Two-Column Note Taking is an organizational structure that will help with reading complex fiction and nonfiction. Rather than use it on a first reading of a text, it might be used effectively when students already have the gist of the piece and are ready to dig deeper for a purpose. The right-hand column helps students remember why they selected a particular word, phrase, or quote.	1, 3

Purpose

Use *during* and *after* reading to

- Create a user-friendly system to record important ideas, related details, and the relationships between concepts.
- Help students remember important points and deepen their understanding of content.
- Help students organize information and thoughts for thinking, writing, studying, or presenting.

Directions

1. Ask students to divide their papers into two columns.
2. Mark the columns with the appropriate headings.

Ideas for Possible Headings

Fiction		Nonfiction	
Column 1	**Column 2**	**Column 1**	**Column 2**
Passage	Response	Main Idea	Detail
Character	Decision	Cause	Effect
Quote	Importance	Concept	Example
		Issue	Connection to Own Life

3. Model how to do the following: In the left-hand column, write a sentence, quote, or cause from the text selection along with the page number. In the right-hand column, write the definition, give an example, list an effect, or explain how the textual evidence you chose impacts meaning or tone or how it supports a central idea in the text.

4. Provide the specific words, quotes, or cause in the left-hand column that you want students to respond to or ask for detail about.

5. Have students complete two-column notes independently, making sure the headings fit the reading or the purpose for reading.

Extensions

Students share their responses with others and solicit feedback.

Students can use two-column notes as study guides, support for writing essays or summaries, or to take notes from films or lectures.

Ask students to write a summary based on the information in their notes.

Two-Column Note-Taking Template

Name: _____

Date: _____

Directions

Fill in the appropriate headings that match your purpose for reading/listening. As you read/listen/view, take two-column notes about important facts, vocabulary, concepts, and other information you want to remember or will need to use.

Topic	
Check one: Lecture ☐ Text ☐ Film ☐ Presentation/Demonstration ☐	

Two-Column Note-Taking Content Examples

Mathematics

Elementary School

When teaching estimating, have students record their estimates in the left column before solving the problem, then write the exact answer in the right column. Comparing the two responses will help them understand if they are making good predictions when they estimate.

Example of Student Notes

Estimated Answer to the Problem	Correct Answer to the Problem
93 + 48 = estimated 90 + 50 = 140	93 + 48 = 141
1,859 – 997 = estimated 2,000 – 1,000 = 1,000	1,859 – 997 = 862

Middle School

Over time, help students take two-column notes from the text readings, showing them how to change the headers according to the specific content.

Examples of Teacher-Selected Headers

Formula	Definition and/or Example

Function	Graph

Problem	Factoring Process

High School

When reviewing how to simplify expressions with equivalent fractions, have students keep two-column notes for the examples used in class so that they will have examples to review while doing homework.

Example of Student Notes

Algebraic Expression	Simplified Expression
$\dfrac{3a^2x}{6a}$	$\dfrac{ax}{2}$
$\dfrac{16\,ab^3c^2}{24ab^2c^5}$	$\dfrac{2b}{3c^3}$

Science

Elementary School

Help students learn to take two-column notes using a mix of text and graphics. As they read an illustrated article on environmental organisms, have them create a list of all of the living and nonliving things mentioned.

Example of Student Notes

Biotic Factors (living things)	Abiotic Factors (nonliving things and factors)
Water lilies	Soil
Frogs	Light
Fish	Temperature

Middle School

After reading each text chapter and completing the related lab or applied task, have students keep a weekly journal to record their understanding of how science changes cause varied effects and reactions.

Example of Student Notes for *Heat Sources*

Cause	Effect/Reaction
Heating fluid in a closed container	Pressure builds up and the fluid boils over
Using a container that is not heat resistant	It may melt or crack when used over heat
Using tongs or test tube clamps	Prevents you from burning your fingers

High School

When studying states of matter in a beginning chemistry class, have students keep a two-column notes journal of examples and characteristics of each state.

Example of Student Notes

State of Matter	Example and Characteristics
Solid	Gold—holds its own shape, high density, and not affected by pressure
Liquid	Water—adopts the shape of its container, high density, and not affected by pressure
Gas	Nitrogen—expands to fill its container, low density, and affected by pressure
Plasma	Interior of the sun—exists only at high temperatures, low density, and depends on pressure

Social Studies

Elementary School

When introducing facts and opinions, create a **Two-Column Note-Taking** chart to help students understand the difference. Have students find two facts in the text selection, enter them, and create an opinion related to each fact. Have students find two opinions in the text, enter them, and create a fact statement related to each opinion.

Middle School

During a world history unit, have students keep a reflection journal to summarize the contributions of famous people throughout history. Have them use their notes to write a report on the attributes and contributions that make a person's legacy stand the test of time.

High School

When studying the Civil War, have students research and compare the American Civil War with a 20th- or 21st-century war to help them understand people's responses to war policy and tactics. As the small groups do their research, have them keep two-column notes that define the similarities or differences between the wars and how the nation responded to them.

Example of Student Notes

American Civil War	Vietnam War
Many Civil War battles were fought on battlefields that were out in the open. The battles themselves were two armies marching toward one another and clashing in the center of the field.	North Vietnamese soldiers used guerrilla warfare methods, such as jungle warfare, as well as women and children for war tasks. Americans were shocked by the guerrilla tactics.
Veterans on both sides were respected after the war, both immediately and long afterward.	U.S. soldiers who fought in Vietnam were not given much respect after their return and fought for many years to be recognized.

English Language Arts

Elementary School

Help students begin to understand inferential thinking by using **Two-Column Note Taking** to identify characters' feelings and the clues from their words or behaviors that hint at them.

Example of Student Notes

Character's Feelings (such as happy, angry, sad)	Clues that Show How the Character Feels (such as words, appearance, or behavior)
Pierre is very frustrated.	He kicked the dirt after dropping the ball. He frowned when his coach said he'd get better with practice.
Tony is mean.	He laughed when Pierre dropped the ball.
The coach is understanding.	He encouraged Pierre. He didn't yell at him.

Middle School

During the study of the epic genre, have students use **Two-Column Note Taking** as they read excerpts from *The Odyssey* to help them understand how Odysseus's internal conflicts related to his external conflicts.

Example of Student Notes

Odysseus's Internal Conflicts	Odysseus's External Conflicts
He refused to run from Cyclops because he wanted to see the caveman.	His refusal got his men angry because they wanted to make a run for it.

High School

After reading a collection of short stories from South Africa, help students connect to very different lifestyles than they've experienced in the United States by responding to unique quotations.

Example of Student Notes for *Somehow Tenderness Survives: Stories of Southern Africa* by Hazel Rochman

Quote and Page Number	Connection (This reminds me of) Question (I wonder) Confusion (I don't understand)
"The cold went through my shirt and shorts." (p. 9)	I thought it was HOT in Africa!
"The white man stares till I lowered my eyes. Well, he said." (p. 18)	The white man demands respect from Les. But not from his own boys. Is it all about color?

Question the Author (QtA)

Description

The **Question the Author (QtA)** strategy asks students to pose questions that interpret and critique what the author is saying, engaging them to construct meaning beyond what the text explicitly states (Beck, McKeown, Hamilton, & Kucan, 1997).

Common Core Connection	Instructional Shift
Question the Author (QtA) is an effective tool for helping students think about the effect of authors' choices. It is especially useful for working with the "craft and structure" cluster of the Reading standards (CCRA.R.4-6).	1

Purpose

Use *during* reading to

- Engage students by deepening their thinking and problem solving while reading.
- Enrich student discussions and interactions with text.
- Support comprehension of difficult but important sections of text.
- Develop metacognitive thinking to monitor and enhance comprehension.

Directions

1. Introduce and discuss the topic of evaluating authors' arguments.

2. Explicitly teach and discuss ideas related to tracing and evaluating authors' arguments and specific claims in a text, including how well the author's claims are supported by reasoning and evidence.

3. Discuss the potential strengths and fallibility of the author in terms of how well the author's overall argument and specific claims are supported by reasoning and evidence.

4. Select a text passage to model the **QtA** process with students, choosing predetermined pause points where you will initiate discussion to question the author's specific claims. For example, share questions you would ask the author about the messages, informational clarity, or relevance and sufficiency of the evidence.

5. Have students generate questions that query the author's specific claims. Discuss what the author is trying to communicate and trace how he or she builds his or her argument. Continue this guided practice with a series of passages across several different texts until most students demonstrate capability of generating meaningful author queries.

6. Ask students to generate their own **QtA** questions during **Paired Reading**, then independent reading. Post a list of example questions to help them get started, while making clear your expectation that they should formulate their own questions as well.

Examples of **QtA** queries:

- What is the author's argument?
- What claims make up the author's argument?
- What evidence does the author provide to support those specific claims?
- How well are the author's claims supported by reasons and evidence?
- What parts of the author's argument feel unsound? Why?

Extension

Combine **QtA** with other literacy support strategies like **Critical Thinking Cue Questions**, **Reciprocal Teaching**, or **Group Summarizing**.

Question the Author (QtA) Template

Name: _____

Date: _____

Reading Selection: _____

What biases does the author express? How do you know?

Your questions for the author

- What is the author's argument?

- What claims make up the author's argument?

- What evidence does the author provide to support those specific claims?

- How well are the author's claims supported by reasons and evidence?

- What parts of the author's argument feel unsound? Why?

Your answers to these questions

Evaluate the author's argument

Adapted from Beck, McKeown, Hamilton, and Kucan (1997).

Question the Author (QtA) Content Examples

English Language Arts *Before* and *during* reading of a new poetry form. Have students use **QtA** as a way to investigate the poem's structure and writing style. Have students pose and answer questions for the author about the number of words or syllables in a line, rhyme scheme, breaks, or literary techniques. Then, as a class, use the answers to students' questions to build a **Frayer Model** of the features of that particular form of poetry.	**Mathematics** *During* a unit on statistics, provide students with two articles reporting polling results. After analyzing the statistics and graphs presented, ask students to use **QtA** to discuss why the two article authors may have represented the statistics in different ways, what the bias or perspective of each author might be, and how that might have influenced the narrative of the article. Discuss how the math could be represented differently to emphasize different points.
Science Provide students with readings that represent two different theories on the reason for the mass extinction that wiped out the dinosaurs. Use **QtA** to engage students in a consideration of the differences among scientific points of view for this topic. Divide students into two groups and give one reading to each. Ask each group to use **QtA** and record answers to their questions on chart paper. Then have the two groups switch articles and repeat the exercise. Use the chart paper responses to engage students in a debate on the issue.	**Social Studies** *During* a unit on the Civil War, provide students with a variety of primary source documents about a single battle or issue. Working in pairs, students can use **QtA** to identify the various points of view represented and then use a graphic organizer to record the key ideas. Have students discuss why these points of view are different. Then ask students to read a section on the same event in a textbook and identify which of the points of view in the primary source documents are represented or are missing. Discuss why this might be the case.

Analytic Graphic Organizers

Why Use Analytic Graphic Organizers?

Current research in learning and brain development confirms what visual learners intuitively understand: Organizing information visually creates new connections to content (Clarke, 1991). It facilitates the development of deeper and more complex schema by structuring information in nonlinear ways. For instance, think about how difficult it would be to teach the location of all of the states in the United States without using a map (Hyerle, 1996)! Although linear representations (like outlines) are very useful in certain contexts, visual consideration, representation, and organization of information allow us to think about things in more elegant, interconnected ways.

What does this mean for you? Helping your students develop proficiency with the use of **Analytic Graphic Organizers (AGOs)** can help them to develop a more sophisticated understanding of text structures and purposes than they may be able to achieve alone. This is great news for you as a teacher because it means that you have a collection of powerful visual tools at your disposal to help your students build background knowledge, develop new information, and extend learning.

Strategy or Worksheet? How to Use Analytic Graphic Organizers

Although **AGOs** are extremely useful tools, their usefulness is determined by the appropriateness of the AGO design to the text or learning purpose of the assignment. The power of the AGO will be maximized by taking these steps:

1. *Define the learning goals for the lesson.* What will students know or be able to do as a result of this lesson?

2. *Analyze the cognitive demands of the text students will read.* What sort of structure does it have? What is its purpose? What is likely to be difficult about it?

3. *Match the goals and demands of the text and the task to the **AGO**.*

4. *Use the gradual release of responsibility model.* Model the use of a new **AGO** and support students while they are learning to use it. Ideally, students will see the value in particular AGOs for particular purposes, and they will choose to use them on their own.

5. *Use the **AGO** once it is completed.* Because so much learning depends on metacognition, think about multiple ways for students to interact with the graphic organizer. Have students share information with one another, complete AGOs in pairs, or create a class AGO for a difficult concept. Bring the graphic organizer out for multiple lessons throughout a unit and challenge students to make additions or changes. Revising an AGO is an excellent formative assessment practice.

Description

An **Analytic Graphic Organizer (AGO)** is a strategy that uses a visual format like charts, diagrams, and graphs to help students explore the characteristics, relationships, or effects of a complex topic. This supports students to organize their thoughts and construct meaning from text. Examples include cause/effect diagrams, comparison/contrast charts, and process flow diagrams.

Common Core Connection	Instructional Shifts
Analytic Graphic Organizers (AGOs), designed carefully and used well, continue to be among the most powerful tools for helping students organize content in order to understand relationships and make new connections. With new, more rigorous, and more specific standards, always keep in mind the standards you are addressing and your instructional purpose as you design your AGO.	1, 2, 3

Purpose

Use *during* and *after* reading to

- Provide a visual way to analyze how information and ideas are linked.
- Help organize information for note taking, learning, and recall.
- Show specific relationships, such as cause/effect, sequence, or comparison/contrast.
- Synthesize information from different locations in the text or from multiple texts.
- Convey understanding of information and concepts so that misconceptions can be seen.

Directions

1. Explain the purpose of using a graphic organizer to visualize how ideas link together.
2. Model how to complete a specific type of graphic organizer before asking students to complete that type in pairs and then individually.
3. After introducing several graphic organizers one at a time, present a variety of graphic organizers together so that students see how the shape of each graphic organizer shows how the information is connected.
4. Model for students how to select a graphic organizer depending on the purpose for organizing information: comparison/contrast, sequence, cause/effect, main idea-supporting detail, pro/con evidence, and so on.
5. Help students select an appropriate graphic organizer.
6. Assist students as needed while they organize the information.
7. Ask students how completing the graphic organizer helped them understand the text differently. Students might discuss this using a **Think-Pair-Share** or complete a **Quick Write** to respond.

Extensions

Have students show their graphic organizers to one another and compare their responses.

Have students design creative variations of graphic organizers to match the content or context.

Have students use their completed graphic organizers as study guides, outlines for essays or other writing, or cue charts for question generating/answering a text; for example: What is the main idea?

What were the turning points in the chapter? What are the important steps in this process?

Analytic Graphic Organizers for Vocabulary Development

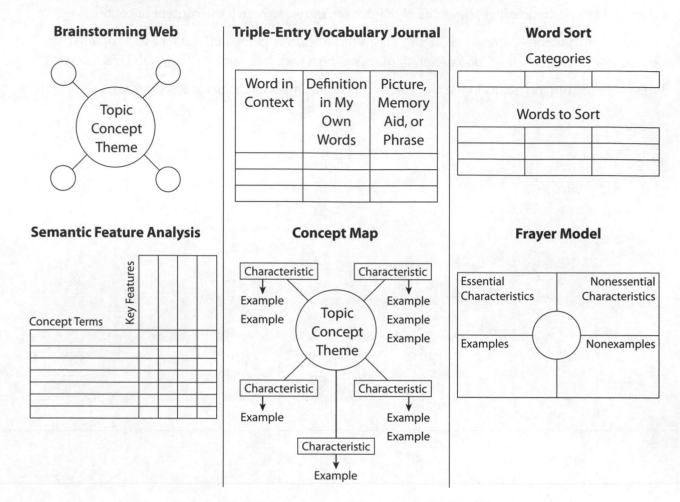

Brainstorming Web

Topic Concept Theme

Triple-Entry Vocabulary Journal

Word in Context	Definition in My Own Words	Picture, Memory Aid, or Phrase

Word Sort

Categories

Words to Sort

Semantic Feature Analysis

Key Features

Concept Terms

Concept Map

Characteristic — Example / Example

Characteristic — Example / Example / Example

Topic Concept Theme

Characteristic → Example

Characteristic → Example / Example

Characteristic → Example

Frayer Model

Essential Characteristics	Nonessential Characteristics
Examples	Nonexamples

Analytic Graphic Organizers for Patterns and Relationships

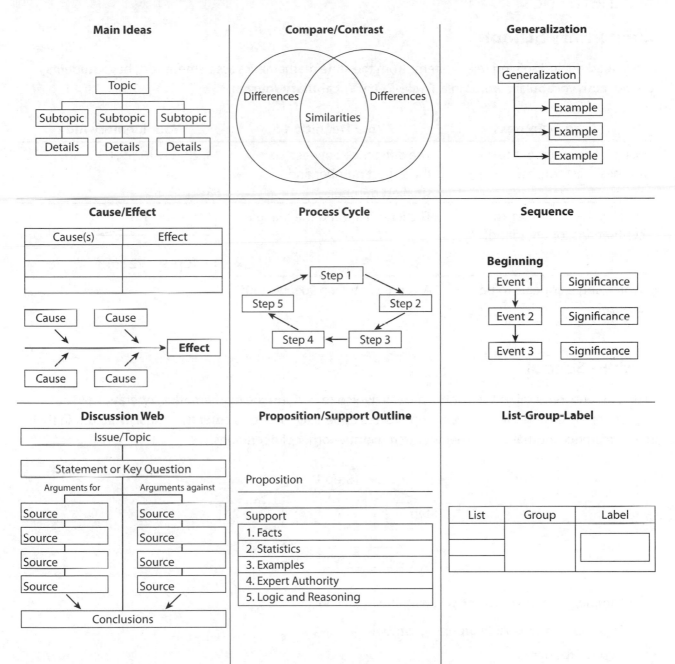

Main Ideas

Topic
- Subtopic — Details
- Subtopic — Details
- Subtopic — Details

Compare/Contrast

Differences / Similarities / Differences

Generalization

Generalization
- Example
- Example
- Example

Cause/Effect

Cause(s)	Effect

Cause, Cause, Cause, Cause → Effect

Process Cycle

Step 1 → Step 2 → Step 3 → Step 4 → Step 5 → Step 1

Sequence

Beginning

Event 1	Significance
Event 2	Significance
Event 3	Significance

Discussion Web

Issue/Topic

Statement or Key Question

Arguments for / Arguments against

Source / Source
Source / Source
Source / Source
Source / Source

Conclusions

Proposition/Support Outline

Proposition

Support
1. Facts
2. Statistics
3. Examples
4. Expert Authority
5. Logic and Reasoning

List-Group-Label

List	Group	Label

Analytic Graphic Organizers Content Examples

Mathematics

Elementary School

While reading and solving release items from the state mathematics assessment test, have students define math vocabulary words in a **Triple-Entry Vocabulary Journal**.

Word in Context	Your Definition	Your Memory Aid
What is the range of the data for these six months?	The difference between the largest number and smallest number.	13, 20, 31, 46, 59, 68 $68 - 13 = 55$
What is the perimeter, in centimeters, of the triangle?	The length around the triangle.	3 ⟋ 10 9 $3 + 10 + 9 = 22$ cm
Which angle appears to be obtuse?	An angle between 90° and 180°.	

Middle School

Help students remember the correct order in which to perform the mathematical operations in an expression by having them make a step process cycle. Have students enter the visual organizer in their math reference journal as another way to remember order of operations.

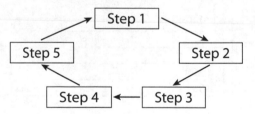

For example, fill in the Process Cycle with the following:

Step 1: Operation inside grouping symbols

Step 2: Exponents

Step 3: Multiplication and division in order from left to right

Step 4: Addition and subtraction in order from left to right

High School

While reading the review section on classification of real and rational numbers, have students use a **Venn diagram** as a visual organizer of the classification of these numbers.

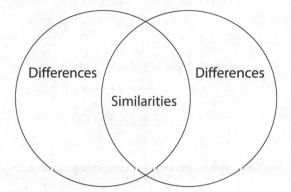

For example, fill in the Venn diagram with the following:

- Write the terms *real and rational numbers* in the *Similarities* section.
- Write in the left side of the *Differences* section the following terms: *integers, whole numbers, natural numbers, odd numbers, even numbers.*
- Write in the right side of the *Differences* section the following terms: *nonintegral numbers, terminating decimals, repeating decimals.*

Science

Elementary School

Help students understand how to support main ideas with evidence by having them create a main idea graphic during reading. Initially, give them the main ideas and gradually let them find the main ideas on their own.

Example of Student Work for the Science Chapter on the Desert

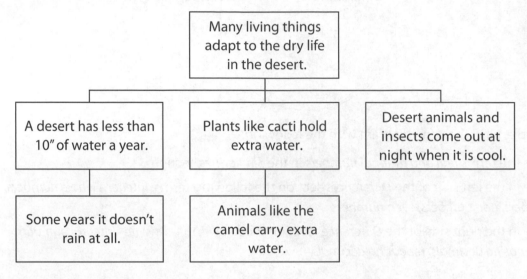

Middle School

In an earth science class, conduct a discovery lab where students look at different minerals while completing a classification graphic organizer of the different characteristics of each.

	Talc	Gypsum	Calcite	Fluorite	Feldspar	Quartz	Topaz
Color							
Luster							
Streak							
Hardness							
Cleavage and Fracture							

Special Properties							

High School

Have students analyze the graphic organization of the Periodic Table of the Elements to answer questions about why the different elements are placed where they are and what the colors, Roman numerals, and numbers mean. Then have them review the website www.visual-literacy.org/pages/documents.htm to see many other ways of graphically organizing information.

Social Studies

Elementary School

During a geography unit on the historical Native Americans of the southwest, have students take notes as they read using a classification graphic organizer.

Native American Group	Land and Climate	Food and Agriculture	Language and Customs	Houses
Hopi	NE Arizona Warm, dry	Raise sheep Vegetable farms	Hopi language Rain dances with snakes	Adobe and stone houses, like apartments
Navajo	NW New Mexico, Arizona, SE Utah Warm, dry	Raise sheep, cattle, and goats Hunt and gather food	Like Apache language Cured sickness with sand painting	Earth and log houses called hogans
Pueblo	N Arizona, W New Mexico Warm, dry	Farming—corn and cotton Hunting	Three languages: Keresan, Tewa, Zuni Dance to get good crops	Mud and stone houses called pueblos

Middle School

To help students understand how much the United States has changed in a short time, have students create a time line of change from 1900 to 2015. Let students pick a topic such as technology, civil rights, animal populations, immigration, or wars.

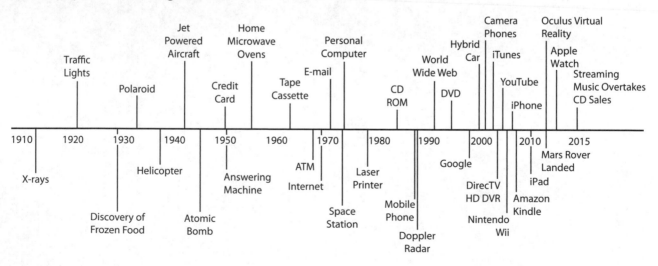

High School

In a review of the federal system in an American history class, have students use their choice of a **Venn diagram** or a **Concept Map** to summarize the key aspects of the division of power between the national government and the states.

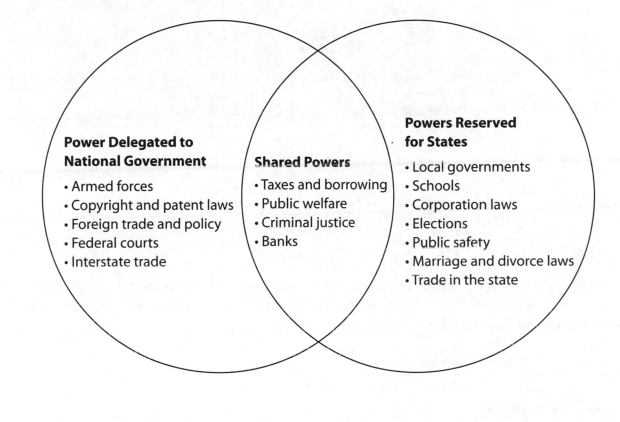

Power Delegated to National Government

- Armed forces
- Copyright and patent laws
- Foreign trade and policy
- Federal courts
- Interstate trade

Shared Powers

- Taxes and borrowing
- Public welfare
- Criminal justice
- Banks

Powers Reserved for States

- Local governments
- Schools
- Corporation laws
- Elections
- Public safety
- Marriage and divorce laws
- Trade in the state

English Language Arts

Elementary School

Use an **Analytic Graphic Organizer** to illustrate the different steps in the writing process.

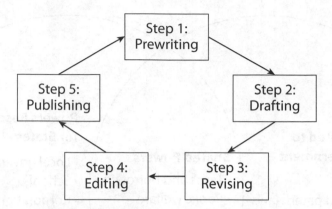

Middle School

During learning about analyzing literature, use an **Analytic Graphic Organizer** to help students make claims and support them with evidence from the text. Example: Lowry, L. (1993). *The giver.* New York, NY: Bantam Books.

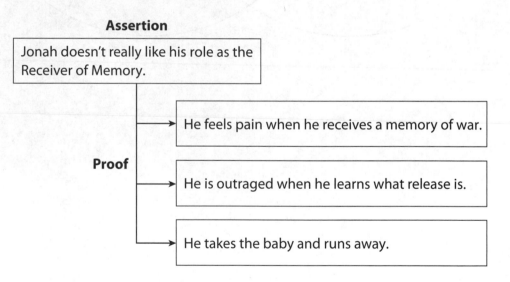

High School

During a study of authors and their work, use an **Analytic Graphic Organizer** to help students think about biographical events authors experience and how those events are reflected in their writing.

Ernest Hemingway

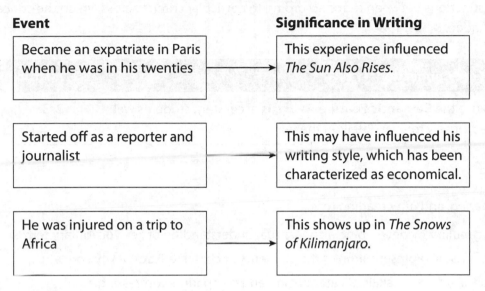

Event

Became an expatriate in Paris when he was in his twenties

Started off as a reporter and journalist

He was injured on a trip to Africa

Significance in Writing

This experience influenced *The Sun Also Rises.*

This may have influenced his writing style, which has been characterized as economical.

This shows up in *The Snows of Kilimanjaro.*

Semantic Feature Analysis

Description

Semantic Feature Analysis is an analytical strategy that helps students examine related concepts by recording distinctions between terms according to particular criteria across which the concepts can be compared (Anders & Bos, 1986).

Common Core Connection	Instructional Shifts
In order to use the **Semantic Feature Analysis** accurately, students will have to read closely for key details in the text.	2, 3

Purpose

Use *before*, *during*, and *after* reading to

- Build vocabulary by developing a conceptual understanding of key vocabulary terms.

- Develop a visual representation of the elements or characteristics of key concepts.

- Develop the analytical skills of categorizing and comparing/contrasting.

- Activate prior knowledge when used *before* reading.

- Assess student understanding when used *during* or *after* reading.

Directions

1. Select a reading that discusses many examples of a single concept, such as a chapter in a content area textbook or a short story with many characters.

2. Select a category of concepts to be analyzed. Examples include types of government, mammals, geometric shapes, human diseases, characters in a play, and ecosystems.

3. Using the **Semantic Feature Analysis** template, list several terms within this concept down the left vertical column. Across the top, list several key features (traits, properties, criteria, or characteristics) associated with any of the examples listed down the left side.

4. Model the process of completing the grid using a **Think-Aloud** to explain your thinking to students as you determine whether to mark a term with a **+**, **–**, or **?**.

5. Have students read the text selection and then code, based on their reading, which key features are associated with which terms. This can be done individually or in pairs. Students should enter a plus sign (**+**) if the term typically possesses that feature, a minus sign (**–**) if the term does not typically include that feature, and a question mark (**?**) if, according to the reading, it is debatable or depends on the specific context or situation whether the feature is applicable.

6. Compare individual or paired responses in small groups. Examine the grid and discuss similarities and differences between the concept terms. If two terms have the same patterns, discuss if there is a feature that differentiates them that could be added to the list.

Extensions

Have students develop generalizations that can be tested against the grid.

Divide the key feature columns into *Before* and *After* so that students can see how their thinking changes when the **Semantic Feature Analysis** is done before and after reading.

Challenge students to come up with different examples and additional key features.

Have students create the concept terms and features on their own, based on the reading.

Semantic Feature Analysis Template

Name: _____

Date: _____

Reading Selection: _____

Topic: _____

Directions

After you read the text selection, code which characteristics are associated with which terms.

Codes

+   = If the term typically possesses that feature

–   = If the term does not typically include that characteristic

?   = If it is debatable or if the key feature depends on the specific context or situation

Concept Terms	Key Features						

Semantic Feature Analysis Content Examples

English Language Arts

After reading narrative, epic, humorous, dramatic, ballad, free verse, and lyric forms of poetry

Help students understand the different literary devices used in different forms of poetry.

	N	E	H	D	B	F	L
Stanzas							
Meter pattern							
Rhyme scheme							
Word repetition							
Accented syllables							
Refrain							
Alliteration							

Mathematics

During reading of trigonometry text chapter on triangles

Use Semantic Feature Analysis to help students understand how various triangles are used in trigonometry to problem-solve real situations.

	Equi-angular	Acute	Obtuse	Right
Distance between various points in the universe				
Projective force and velocity				
Electric circuits				
Architectural design				
Light refraction				

Science

Before, during, and *after* reading about systems of the body

Help students determine the interrelationships (or not) of human systems that impact health.
Systems codes:
S = Skeletal M = Muscular E = Endocrine
C = Cardiovascular D = Digestive U = Urinary
L = Lymphatic R = Respiratory N = Nervous

	S	M	E	C	D	U	L	R	N
Fitness									
Heart									
Cancer									
Diabetes									
Obesity									
Liver									
Alzheimer's									

Social Studies

Before, during, and *after* reading about economic systems in various countries and their impacts on the average citizen

Use Semantic Feature Analysis to predict and confirm the impact of elements of economic systems in various countries upon its people.

	US	Can	Mex	GB	Jap	Chi	Iraq
Employment							
Healthcare							
Retirement							
Recreation							
Education							
Agriculture							
Cultural arts							

Discussion Web (Social Studies)

Description

A **Discussion Web** is an **Analytic Graphic Organizer** that works particularly well with controversial topics—it promotes critical thinking by encouraging students to take a position. The strategy requires students to establish and support evidence for their selected positions based on their reading of narrative or expository texts (adapted from Duthie, 1986).

Common Core Connection	Instructional Shift
In the CCSS, students are expected to express an opinion on a topic or make a claim and support it with evidence. Most real-world topics don't clearly invite us to be "for" and "against" but rather to make more nuanced arguments. The **Discussion Web** template will work best when preparing to debate a topic that has clear pro and con sides.	2

Purpose

Use *during* or *after* reading one or more texts to

- Provide a framework for analyzing an issue by citing evidence for or against an issue.
- Develop students' ability to draw conclusions based on evidence, not opinion.
- Provide opportunities for active discussion and collaboration.
- Help students organize ideas for writing and use evidence to support their points of view.
- Encourage the use of multiple resources to determine a conclusion.
- Help students refine their thinking by listening to opposing information or ideas.

Directions

1. Choose, or have students choose, an issue with opposing viewpoints.
2. Locate, or have students locate, a variety of resources that describe the issue.
3. Provide, or have students create, a guiding question to focus the discussion.
4. Have students work alone or in pairs to complete both sides of the **Discussion Web**, note text title and page numbers where they found the evidence, and form a tentative conclusion. Encourage them to be open-minded and suspend their personal judgments during data collection.
5. Have two pairs work together to review their **Discussion Webs** and add additional arguments. Have the four students discuss all of the evidence and come to consensus about the strongest point of view, based on the evidence (not personal opinion).

6. Have students create a conclusion that summarizes the group's thinking and write it at the bottom of the **Discussion Web**. Encourage them to avoid biased language.

7. Have each small group report their conclusions to the whole class. They should mention any dissenting viewpoints within their groups. Limit the report to 3 minutes so that all groups have time to present.

8. Have each student review his or her own tentative conclusion about the guiding question and then complete a one-paragraph **Quick Write** that states the conclusion, citing the three to five key facts or reasons that support the conclusion.

Extensions

Have students write a response supporting the opposite point of view.

Have students conduct a formal debate or "town meeting" discussion. If possible, present to an authentic audience and solicit feedback.

Discussion Web Template

Name: _____

Date: _____

Issue/Topic

Statement or Key Question

Arguments for   Arguments against

Source:		Source:

Source:		Source:

Source:		Source:

Source:		Source:

Conclusions

Discussion Web Content Examples

Social Studies

Elementary School

After reading about issues in the local community, have students identify possible stances on one of the issues. Then utilize the **Discussion Web** template as a way to scaffold students' efforts to support their opinions with evidence from the reading.

Middle School

After reading opinions on the tension between the rights and responsibilities of U.S. citizens, introduce several issues that address this notion and have students work in pairs to read more sources and develop opposing viewpoints on their chosen issues.

High School

Before reading about Supreme Court cases that deal with the concept of legitimate power, have students read introductory information and choose one of the cases. Groups can develop opposing arguments they will use to debate the issue for another class.

Proposition/Support Outline (Science)

Description

The **Proposition/Support Outline** is an **Analytic Graphic Organizer** that asks students to set forth a hypothesis or proposition and list the arguments and evidence from the text to support or refute the statement. It is particularly effective when used with science content.

Common Core Connection	Instructional Shifts
Substitute the word *claim* for *proposition* to align with the CCSS language. Students will identify or create claims, find evidence, and develop their conclusions with reasoning. The **Proposition/Support Outline** AGO reminds students that there are different kinds of evidence that can support a claim.	2, 3

Purpose

Use *before*, *during*, and *after* reading to

- Develop higher-order critical thinking skills, particularly analysis and evaluation.

- Help students focus during reading as they look for supporting arguments and draw conclusions.

- Help students separate fact and opinion in a reading selection and analyze the justification given to support conclusions or generalizations.

- Help students identify information that reflects opinion, bias, personal viewpoints, hypotheses, and debatable assumptions or assertions.

Directions

1. Introduce the term *proposition* as a statement that can be argued as true.

2. Discuss fact and opinion. Brainstorm examples and have students offer criteria for separating fact and opinion.

3. Test the student criteria using the list of proposition statements for students to identify as fact or opinion.

4. Assign a reading selection that features one or more strong propositions and have small groups of students identify the key propositions of the selection.

5. Have student groups then evaluate each of these statements, looking for evidence of opinion, bias, or personal viewpoints.

6. Have student groups identify the statement as fact or opinion after taking notes that describe the supporting evidence: facts, statistics, examples, expert authority, logic, and reasoning. (These can be put on a graphic organizer chart.)

7. Have the groups share their conclusions with the whole class. Encourage further discussion of any statement about which the groups cannot agree.

Extensions

Use the **Proposition/Support Outline** for independent research so that students scrutinize reference materials for relevant information and arguments.

Have students write a position paper or analyze multimedia information related to a proposition, supporting it with appropriate facts, statistics, examples, expert authority, and logic/reasoning.

Proposition/Support Outline Template

Name: _____

Date: _____

Topic Name: _____

Proposition Name: _____

1. Facts/Statistics	Source

2. Examples	Source

3. Expert Authority	Source

4. Conclusions (based on logical reasoning, not just preference/opinion)	

Based on Buehl (2009).

Proposition/Support Outline Content Examples

Science

Elementary School

Use the **Proposition/Support Outline** during a unit on environmental change to help students sift through the competing opinions on the impact of humans on the environment. As a class, use the *gradual release of responsibility model* to teach students how to use the strategy. Put students in pairs and provide each pair with a different reading on an issue the class is studying. Have them work in pairs to complete the outlines and then discuss their findings with other groups of students. Collect the opinions of the different articles and debate those positions.

Middle School

Use the **Proposition/Support Outline** to engage students in a consideration of different points of view on any controversial topic, such as whether the United States should eliminate its use of fossil fuels. Have students work in groups or individually to complete outlines on different readings around the same topic. Use **Two-Column Note Taking** to have students keep track of each article and the strength of the proposition in each. Then use this information to have students write a short essay on the position, determining their own positions and using the information from each of the articles as support.

High School

Have students use **Proposition/Support Outlines** to analyze information from multimedia sources as well as traditional text on an issue under investigation by the class, such as the use of stem cells in medical research. Have students search for three different high-quality, Web-based sources of information, using the outlines to determine the extent to which each source effectively supports its position. Then, have students work in two groups to identify the different points of view represented on the topic and stage a debate between the two different positions.

Inference Notes Wheel (English Language Arts)

Description

The **Inference Notes Wheel** is an **Analytic Graphic Organizer** that is particularly useful in the English language arts classroom. The graphic organizer asks students to record literal (in the text) information about a topic or person in the inside wedges and inferential interpretations in the outer wedges of a circle to help students draw tentative conclusions from cues in text (adapted from Burke, 2002).

Common Core Connection	Instructional Shift
The **Inference Notes Wheel** helps students get at CCRA.R.1: "Read closely to understand what the text says explicitly and to make logical inferences from it; cite specific textual evidence when writing or speaking to support conclusions drawn from the text."	2

Purpose

Use *during* and *after* reading to

- Draw inferences about what is not directly stated or observable.

- Understand literal statements may contain inferential clues that require interpretation by the reader.

- Understand that evidence-based inferences and conclusions result from information in the text that can be cited.

Directions

1. Prior to the lesson, identify a reading selection that requires inferential thinking in several cases to develop full understanding of what the text is saying about a topic or person.

2. Choose six quotes from the selection that relate to a specific topic or person and place them in the inner wedges of the **Inference Notes Wheel**. Complete one or two of the inferential responses to model what an inferential response contains.

3. Begin instruction by discussing how inferences are derived from literal information.

   Examples:

   - It is cloudy outside. What might happen? (snow, rain, or stay cloudy)

   - The man was frowning and his arms were crossed. What might he be feeling? (anger, frustration, confusion, shyness, or discomfort)

4. Brainstorm context cues or patterns students can use to know when inferential thinking is required. Examples:

   - Adjectives or adverbs provide a clue about emotions or possible action.
   - A list or several pieces of information close in the text lead to a generalization.
   - A description of a setting can be used to create a mood.
   - A metaphor or symbol can be used to describe a person's character or probable action.

5. Have students work in pairs or small groups to discuss and complete the rest of the **Inference Notes Wheel** for the passage.

6. When the **Inference Notes Wheel** is complete, have students write a summary conclusion about the topic or person and support their analyses with quotes and citations from the text.

7. Continue to have students use the **Inference Notes Wheel** with other text passages and gradually have them select the literal information on their own.

Extension

After reading, have students list inferences they derived from text, insert them in the outer wedges of the **Inference Notes Wheel**, and add supporting quotes that support the conclusion.

Inference Notes Wheel Template

Name: _____

Date: _____

Directions

Find six statements, examples, or quotations in the text that directly relate to the topic or character listed in the center of the wheel (or use one chosen by the teacher). Selected quotations or statements should suggest to the reader an inference beyond the literal statement in the text. Place one statement in each of the inner circle wedges and note the page number where each is found. In the outer wedge, explain your inference about each statement based on the cues in the text.

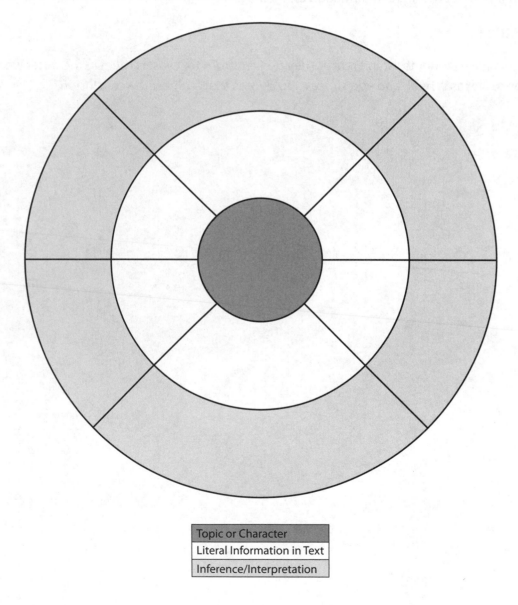

Topic or Character
Literal Information in Text
Inference/Interpretation

Conclusion

Summarize the inferences you made about the topic or character, based on the six inferential statements, and explain how your analysis was based on the evidence in the text. Use direct quotations or citation information to support your reasoning.

Inference Notes Wheel Content Examples

English Language Arts

Elementary School

While reading *Bud, Not Buddy* by Christopher Paul Curtis, use the **Inference Notes Wheel** to help students develop an understanding of inference and how to think about indirect presentation of character traits.

Character: Bud

Quote: "We were all standing in line for breakfast when one of the caseworkers came in and tap-tap-tapped down the line."

Inference: The narrator is living in an orphanage.

Middle School

During and *after* reading *Autumn Street* by Lois Lowry, have students use the **Inference Notes Wheel** to build their ability to support their ideas. Work with them to develop propositions about the text. Have them place these in the outer circle. Then, have them identify quotes that support those propositions in the middle circle.

Topic: The effect of World War II on families in the United States

Quote: "Pearl Harbor is on the radio, Daddy," I told him, "And Mama is crying." After that, the answer to everything was "Because of the War." After that, there were air raid drills at kindergarten. We had to run, holding hands, to the subway station and hide there. Because of the war.

Inference: Pearl Harbor led to a great deal of fear in America.

High School

During the study of complex texts, use **Inference Notes Wheels** to examine different aspects of a text. Use these as prewriting for a longer essay or paper about the novel. For example, while studying F. Scott Fitzgerald's *The Great Gatsby,* complete Inference Notes Wheels either on several different characters or on several aspects of one of the main characters. Use each wheel as the basis for one section of a longer paper.

Character: Jay Gatsby

Quote: "That huge place there?" she cried pointing. "Do you like it?" "I love it, but I don't see how you live there all alone."

"I keep it always full of interesting people, night and day. People who do interesting things. Celebrated people."

Inference: Gatsby craved the company of rich and powerful people.

Think-Pair-Share

Description

Think-Pair-Share is a cooperative discussion strategy that emphasizes what students should do at each of the three steps of the protocol: think, pair, and share (Lyman, 1981).

Common Core Connection	Instructional Shifts
CCRA.SL.1: "Prepare for and participate effectively in a range of conversations and collaborations with diverse partners, building on others' ideas and expressing their own clearly and persuasively." **Think-Pair-Share** is a strategy that stands the test of time: It is as simple and powerful as ever for helping students solidify their own ideas and learn from others' ideas.	1, 2, 3

Purpose

Use *before*, *during*, or *after* reading to

- Allow for reflection and sharing before whole-group discussion.
- Provide time for everyone to formulate responses to the reading, experience, or prompt.

Directions

1. Create a question, prompt, or problem to generate student thinking.
2. Have students spend 2–3 minutes brainstorming or thinking individually about the question asked or problem posed. Option: Have students do a **Quick Write** of their thoughts.
3. Have students share their ideas with a partner for 2–3 minutes.
4. Have students share their most significant ideas with the whole group, taking care to not repeat what someone else has already reported.

Extensions

Stop at a planned point during an interactive read-aloud and have students **Think-Pair-Share** about a possible solution to the character's problem, a prediction about what might happen next, or supporting detail about a content concept.

Schedule **Think-Pair-Shares** during silent reading to stimulate thinking and interaction with text.

Use **Think-Pair-Share** as a strategy to enhance active listening during lectures, presentations, or demonstrations.

Think-Pair-Share Template

Name: _____

Date: _____

Directions

Write the question or problem in the following space.

Think

Write three answers or ideas you have about this question or problem.

1.

2.

3.

Pair

Discuss your ideas with a partner. Check any ideas above that your partner also wrote down. Write down ideas your partner had that you did not.

1.

2.

3.

Share

Review all of your ideas and circle the one you think is most important. One of you will share this idea with the whole group. As you listen to the ideas of others, write down three you liked.

1.

2.

3.

Think-Pair-Share Content Examples

English Language Arts

Before learning about writing for specific audiences

Brainstorm a list of different types of books and the people who might read each type. Then introduce the **Think-Pair-Share** activity, using the protocol to address the following question: "How do books look and sound different when they are written for different audiences?"

Once pairs have completed their discussions, draw two columns on the board or digital display. Ask each pair to share an important point but to be careful not to repeat the same point shared by another group.

Write each pair's most important idea on the board in the left column. In the right column, have students suggest other similar examples.

Use this information to begin a class discussion about keeping your audience in mind when writing.

Mathematics

Before and *during* reading an introduction on probability

Pose the following question: How do you make decisions? Ask students to do a **Quick Write** of their thoughts about this and then turn and share their ideas with a partner for 2–3 minutes.

Ask each pair to share the similarities and differences in decision-making approaches. Record this information on chart paper and ask students to keep these in mind as they read the introduction.

After reading, have students think about how their decision-making processes might or might not be influenced by statistics. Then have students pair to discuss and then share with the class. This builds background knowledge for the forthcoming unit.

Science

Before a lesson sequence about the phases of the moon

Post the following questions and have students record their ideas using the **Think-Pair-Share** protocol:

1. Think on your own: What do you think causes the phases of the moon? How are moon phases different from eclipses?

2. Pair with a partner to discuss.

3. Share the most important ideas you discussed with the whole group.

After studying the phases through direct observation, modeling, and readings, have students return to this record of their initial thinking and make corrections to anything that may have been incorrect in their original explanations.

Social Studies

During a unit on leaders of the civil rights movement

Use **Think-Pair-Share** at various points as a way to help students consolidate their learning, review material, and generate questions.

For example, divide the class into groups and assign each group one key civil rights leader. Ask students to read the section in the book on their leaders and to do some online research about the person, jotting notes as they read.

In each group, ask students to complete the Think-Pair-Share protocol in reference to their assigned leaders. Have students think about the most interesting and important facts they learned about this person and then to share them with the small group. Then ask each group to share with the class.

Record the results on the board or digital display and use them as a way to discuss the differences among these leaders with students.

Reciprocal Teaching

Description

Reciprocal Teaching is a collaborative routine for improving reading comprehension. Four-person teams use the skills of summarizing, questioning, clarifying, and predicting to bring meaning to the text (Palincsar & Brown, 1984).

Common Core Connection	Instructional Shifts
To be used effectively, **Reciprocal Teaching** must be modeled and practiced. The goal of this collaborative tool is for students to be able to use independently the metacognitive strategies they are learning as a group. This is a very effective strategy to support weaker readers. Be sure to insist that your "predictors" base their predictions on evidence from the text.	1, 3

Purpose

Use *during* reading to

- Improve students' skills at summarizing, questioning, clarifying, and predicting.
- Help struggling readers practice the habits and skills of strong readers.
- Encourage collaborative exploration of text.

Directions

1. Create groups of four students.
2. Distribute one note card to each group member identifying each person's role:
   - Summarizer
   - Questioner
   - Clarifier
   - Predictor
3. Have students silently read a few paragraphs of the assigned text selection. Encourage them to use note-taking strategies such as selective underlining or sticky notes to help them better prepare for their roles in the discussion.
4. At a given stopping point, the Summarizer will highlight key ideas up to this point in the reading.
5. The Questioner will then pose questions about the selection.
6. The Clarifier addresses confusing parts and attempts to answer the questions.
7. The Predictor can offer guesses about what the author will tell the group next.

8. The roles in the group then switch one person to the right, and the next selection is read. Students repeat the process using their new roles. This continues until the entire selection is read.

It is important to teach, model, and practice each role before expecting students to do all four together.

Possible Verbal Prompts

Summarizer	The important ideas in what I read are
Questioner	What connections can I make? How does this information change what I was thinking? What is the author telling me by this comment?
Clarifier	I do not understand the part where
	I need to know more about
Predictor	I think_____, I wonder_____, I predict_____

Extensions

Use with **Paired Reading** or **Save the Last Word for Me**.

Have students write individual summaries after they finish reading and discussing the selection together.

Reciprocal Teaching Template

Name: _____

Date: _____

Directions

Read the selection and take notes on the four comprehension strategies in preparation for the **Reciprocal Teaching** group activity.

Summarize

_____

Question

_____

Clarify

_____

Predict

_____

Reciprocal Teaching Content Examples

English Language Arts

During small-group reading of a novel, play, short story, or other genre

Adapt Literature Circle roles to the four roles of **Reciprocal Teaching**, rotating them at appropriate pause points in the text reading and specifying areas of focus to deepen the discussion past literal interpretation; use Horacio Quiroga's *The Alligator War* as an example.

Summarizer: Parallel the alligator behaviors to people's behaviors during the summary.

Questioner: Ask only questions that require inferential thinking.

Clarifier: Be the wise old alligator when you respond to the questions.

Predictor: Compare human beings to alligators in predicting what will happen if a warship again goes up the river.

Mathematics

During small-group completion of college entrance exam practice tests

Involve students in actively discussing the types of exam questions and techniques for answering them by applying the **Reciprocal Teaching** roles to the sample questions.

Summarizer: State numerical math problems in words or word problems in numbers and symbols.

Questioner: Ask about vocabulary or process steps to solve the problem.

Clarifier: Explain vocabulary or process steps.

Predictor: Predict that the detractor answer the test makers include is easy to select if the problem isn't carefully thought out.

Science

During reading of a difficult chemistry chapter on chemical equilibrium and Le Chatelier's Principle

Have students take on the four roles of *Summarizer, Questioner, Clarifier*, and *Predictor* after reading each of the sections. Have each role focus on specific content when reading.

Summarizer: Focus on the opening and closing paragraphs of each one- to two-page section.

Questioner: Read the Section Review Questions and ask the group any you don't understand yourself.

Clarifier: Review the graphs and figures that explain the reactions.

Predictor: Read the sample problems and Chemistry in Action tips to predict why it matters for students to understand chemical equilibrium.

Social Studies

Before, during, and *after* reading a chapter on problems of the presidency with the case study of Watergate

Ask small groups of students to compare the president's problems during Watergate with the problems of today's president, focusing on the theme: Does the president have too many jobs and too much power?

Have students guide their discussions by taking on the four roles of **Reciprocal Teaching**: *Summarizer, Questioner, Clarifier*, and *Predictor*.

Paired Reading

Description

Paired Reading is a combined reading comprehension and fluency strategy that supports students to be actively involved in the structured reading aloud of a shared text. Students benefit from the intensive sessions of reading, speaking, and active listening.

Common Core Connection	Instructional Shift
This collaborative strategy supports many standards but especially CCRA.R.2. (summary). During **Paired Reading** teachers can also observe independent reading skills, monitor for understanding, and offer support.	1

Purpose

Use *during* reading to

- Give students practice in oral reading and build fluency.

- Provide practice with active listening, reading aloud, and summarizing.

- Promote active engagement with reading.

- Develop specific skills related to reading comprehension.

Directions

1. Basic **Paired Reading** requires establishing ground rules about when and how help will be asked for or offered when reading, how turns will be taken, and what each role will include. One basic set of ground rules might be the following:

    - In pairs, take turns reading a paragraph at a time from an assigned reading.

    - The reader reads in a low voice, loud enough only for the listener to hear.

    - When the reader completes the paragraph, the listener provides a summary of the paragraph that needs to be "approved" by the reader. If the summary is not clear or accurate, the pair goes back to the text and rereads silently to add what is necessary.

    - Then the two switch roles, with the first reader becoming the active listener and summarizer.

    - If the reader stumbles on a word or is having difficulty, the reader can ask for help from the partner. If help is not asked for, then the listener should give the reader the opportunity to figure it out.

2. Give directions for what the pair should do when they finish reading. Possible options include:

    - Discussing what they each found interesting about what they have read

    - Answering questions or completing a graphic organizer together or separately

- Interviewing another pair about their reading session (what went well/what did not)
- Asking pairs to contribute three interesting words (or words that meet specific criteria) from their reading to the **Interactive Word Wall**
- Adding to their learning log or journal based on what was read
- Asking partners to write a collaborative summary of what they read

Extensions

Extend the listening/summarizing role to include clarifying, predicting, and questioning.

Let readers read longer segments of the text before switching roles.

Give pairs a set of cards that direct them to do different things with the text: visualize, clarify, or make a connection. The listener picks a card before the reader begins to read and then shares according to the card after the reader completes the section.

Paired Reading Content Examples

English Language Arts

After viewing the video and *during* the reading of Shakespeare's *As You Like It*

Model for students how to do a **Paired Reading** using Jacques's speech, *The Seven Ages of Man*. Show students how they are to summarize the plot actions and the ways character actions and dialogue show how the character feels about life.

Then have students do Paired Readings intermittently throughout the reading of the play to help them comprehend difficult sections.

Mathematics

During reading of review information about algebraic expressions prior to the unit on functions and graphs

Use **Paired Readings** to have students read and summarize the text pages on addition, subtraction, multiplication, and division of algebraic expressions. Ask students to focus their summaries on defining the related math terms and recognizing an example when mathematically represented in numbers and symbols.

Science

During a reading about Newton's Second Law of Motion

After a lesson sequence about the Second Law of Motion, have students do a **Paired Reading** to summarize a text explanation of Newton's Second Law with the key outcome of understanding

- The inversely proportional relationship of acceleration and mass
- The predicted results when acceleration, net force, or mass changes

Social Studies

Before, during, and *after* reading about Roosevelt's New Deal

Have pairs of students read about the New Deal in a variety of texts or online resources. Stress that during their summary responses, students should focus on learning how the New Deal would impact American life in relation to the following:

- Labor and employment
- Housing
- Business and the economy
- Farm programs and rural life
- Retirement

Critical Thinking Cue Questions

Description

Critical Thinking Cue Questions related to the skills in Bloom's Taxonomy are purposely constructed to ensure that students are stimulated to respond at all levels of the cognitive domain, especially the higher levels. Students may be asked to respond through **Quick Writes**, learning logs, tests, creative writing that answers the six prompts, **Role-Audience-Format-Topic (RAFT)** activities, or other writing or speaking activities.

Common Core Connection	Instructional Shift
Critical Thinking Cue Questions are especially helpful for creating text-dependent questions that scaffold students through several rounds of close reading, working from more concrete to more complex questions. Using higher-order thinking skills also helps students climb the "staircase of complexity," completing more challenging tasks with text of increasing complexity.	1

Purpose

Use *before*, *during*, and *after* reading to

- Establish a purpose for reading.
- Help students develop their thinking skills at all levels of cognition.
- Ensure that learning assignments respond to all levels of cognition.
- Deepen student comprehension of text, especially at the higher levels.
- Stimulate original thinking through the use of open-ended questions.
- Provide an array of questions to support students to demonstrate what they have learned.

Directions

1. Assess the cognitive demands of the reading assignment to determine which of the six levels of thinking are required for students to understand what they are reading.

2. Explicitly teach students about **Critical Thinking Cue Questions** and share a copy of the cue questions with them.

3. Develop questions in advance about the text and give them to students before they read to provide a purpose for engaging with the text.

4. Model how to respond to Bloom's thinking levels through **Think-Alouds**, whole-group discussions, small-group discussions, paired answers, and other methods to learn how to answer questions at the six levels.

5. Once students are comfortable with the six levels of thinking skills, assign independent after-reading tasks using questions from the chart.

Extensions

Provide choice for student responses by offering several questions from which they select one to answer for each of the six levels.

Have students use the chart when previewing text before they read to set their own purposes for reading.

Ask students to construct questions and answers about what they have read, using the cue questions on the chart.

Note:

While these cues typically apply where shown on the display, the context of the complete question or passage may change the cognitive demand in some cases.

Six Levels of Critical Thinking Cue Questions

Based on Bloom's Taxonomy

Lower-Order Thinking Skills			Higher-Order Thinking Skills		
1. REMEMBER	**2. UNDERSTAND**	**3. APPLY**	**4. ANALYZE**	**5. EVALUATE**	**6. CREATE**
• Called	• Define	• Action	• Allow, not allow, criteria	• Advantages	• Adapt
• Describe	• Discuss	• Apply	• Analyze, assess	• Affect	• Alternative
• How many	• Example	• Assemble	• But, except, exception	• Agree	• Change, substitute
• Identify	• Explain	• Build a model	• Cause	• Appraise	• Could
• Is, are	• How	• Calculate	• Check	• Appropriate	• Create
• Label	• Locate	• Construct	• Classify, organize	• Assess	• Elaborate
• List	• Mean	• Demonstrate	• Compare, contrast	• Better, best (-er, -est words)	• Formulate
• Memorize	• Paraphrase	• Do, be done	• Conclude, conclusion	• Choose	• Imagine
• Name	• Restate	• Dramatize	• Correct, proper, incorrect	• Consider	• Improve
• Recall	• Summarize	• Draw	• Determine, diagnose, suspect	• Criticize	• Invent
• Recognize	• Translate	• Duplicate, reproduce	• Difference, differs	• Defend	• Maximize
• Repeat	• Visualize	• Function		• Disagree	• Minimize
• Select		• Give example		• Evaluate	• Modify
• State		• Illustrate		• Importance	• Predict
• What, what is/are/does		• Operate		• Judge	• Propose alternative
• When		• Perform		• Justify	• Put it all together
• Where		• Plan, prepare		• Opinion	• Synthesize
• Which		• Procedure		• Optimum	
• Who					

- Theorize
- What could be
- What if

- Perception, perspective
- Prioritize
- Probable
- Prove, disprove
- Rate, rank
- Recommend, suggest
- Support
- Value, quality
- What could this mean

- Distinguish, differentiate
- Divide, break apart
- Evidence
- Examine
- Failure
- Idea, concept
- Identify, indicate
- If, if/then
- Infer
- Like, unlike
- Logical
- Makes
- Needs
- Next, next step
- Observe
- Pattern
- Predict, hypothesize
- Prevent, precaution
- Priority
- Problem, situation
- Process

- Proper, acceptable
- Schedule
- Show
- Sketch
- Solve
- Use, employ
- Visualize
- Write

- Fill-in-the-missing-word sentences

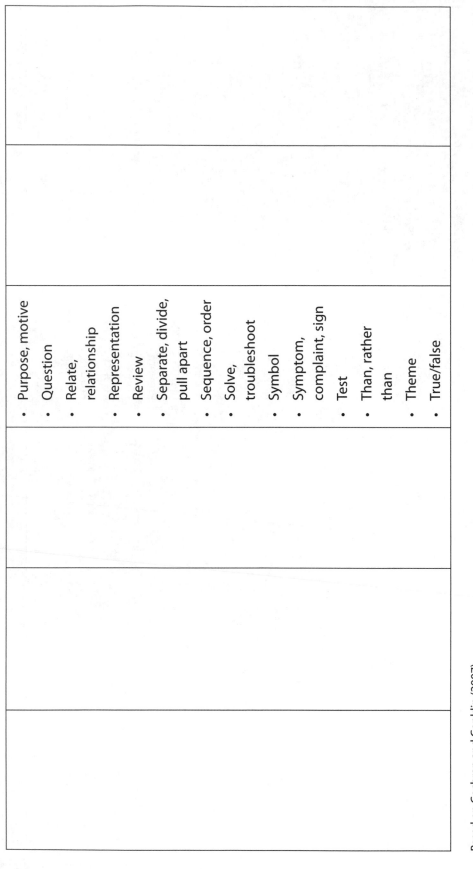

- Purpose, motive
- Question
- Relate, relationship
- Representation
- Review
- Separate, divide, pull apart
- Sequence, order
- Solve, troubleshoot
- Symbol
- Symptom, complaint, sign
- Test
- Than, rather than
- Theme
- True/false

Based on Cochran and Conklin (2007).

Critical Thinking Cue Questions Content Examples

English Language Arts

During and *after* reading a classic novel with complex plot, characterization, and theme

During reading, provide cue questions for students to respond at all cognitive levels: knowledge, comprehension, application, analysis, evaluation, synthesis.

After reading, provide a chart of cue questions for each of the six types of critical thinking levels and have students create and answer questions to communicate their learning.

Mathematics

Before and after reading a text chapter on measurement

Before reading, students activate prior knowledge and predict what will be learned by answering six 1-minute **Quick Write** prompts that relate to precision, accuracy, and units of measurement. Each question is based on one of the six levels of Bloom's Critical Thinking Taxonomy.

After reading, review and revise the predictive responses to demonstrate understanding of how precision, accuracy, and measurement units affect mathematical predictions and estimates.

Science

During reading of a text chapter, reviewing graphic depictions, and viewing a video on plate tectonics

Structure a **Two-Column Note-Taking** chart with prompts that require students to analyze, evaluate, and synthesize information on plate tectonics and correlate it with geological features in today's world.

Social Studies

Before, during, and, *after* reading editorials about the economic systems in several countries

Have students write a persuasive essay about the country they think has the most effective economic system and justify the response by analytical comparisons, evaluative judgments about quality, and a synthesizing description about how other countries would benefit from adopting the economic system.

Use of *Coding/Comprehension Monitoring* in an Elementary Social Studies Classroom

Mr. Yuan was concerned because he knew that many of his students had scored at somewhat low Lexile levels on the school's reading assessment. He'd heard from Ms. Carson, a fourth-grade teacher, that use of the **Coding/Comprehension Monitoring** strategy helped her struggling readers think about and learn from text. He did a quick online search for some articles and sample lesson plans about Coding to make sure he knew how to teach this strategy. Then he began to plan his unit on Europeans Exploring America.

Before Reading/Learning

The next day his students seemed mildly curious when they came back from lunch and saw that each American history book had a small stack of brightly colored sticky notes on the top right corner. Once the class settled down, Mr. Yuan opened with a question.

"How many of you have ever sailed or been out in a boat?" Only three students raised their hands. There were very few lakes nearby and most students had never seen the ocean. Mr. Yuan realized they'd need a lot of support to understand the difficulties the Europeans had experienced when they first sailed across to America. "But you know what boats look like, right?" Some students nodded but looked puzzled, wondering what the point was of this discussion.

"Open your book to page 30 and see if the pictures look like any boat you've ever seen." Most students shook their heads when they saw the old-fashioned boats with large masts and sails.

"We're going to read in a different way today and here's what you're going to do. Every time you see something in a picture or in the text that is like something you've personally seen, I want you to mark a sticky note with a check mark. When you see something you've never seen or heard much about before, I want you to place a sticky note right at that line or picture with an X on it. So take your first sticky note and put it by the picture of that sailboat and mark it with a check mark or an X."

He walked around as students placed the notes, seeing that only Tanisha used a check mark. "Tanisha, you've seen this type of boat before?"

"Yes, Mr. Yuan. Last year we went up to Plymouth and they had a big boat there, the *Mayflower 2*."

Mr. Yuan smiled, "Yes, that's a replica of the one the Pilgrims used. Does anyone know what a replica is?"

"Like a fake?" asked Tim.

"Well, it is not the original. But it is meant to be exactly like the original. So, in a sense, it is a fake. But the purpose is to show as closely as possible what the original was like. So the boat Tanisha saw was a replica of the original *Mayflower*. Okay! Now here's how I want you to mark text when you read."

Jamie raised his hand. "I know what you're doing, Mr. Yuan," he said. You're teaching us Coding. I already know how."

"Great," responded Mr. Yuan. "Come on up and help me show the others. Anyone else want to help teach Coding with Jamie and me?" Several students shook their heads no, but Bernard jumped up.

During Reading/Learning

Mr. Yuan explained that today they'd be reading Unit 2, Europeans Explore America. "Would you like to read alone, in pairs, or as a whole class together?" he asked. Most students replied pairs, so he asked them to quickly form their pairs. While they all moved, he showed Jamie and Bernard how he had planned to model Coding for the first two pages. "So listen up—Jamie and Bernard are the teachers now."

Jamie began. "Well, I like it. What Coding does is help you pay attention to what you read."

Bernard chimed in, "And it sure helps a lot 'cause you all know I can't read too well and here I am, teaching you!"

Mr. Yuan nodded proudly, noting no one snickered when Bernard admitted he wasn't the best reader. Mr. Yuan constantly emphasized that learning to improve reading requires practice and exercise of the brain, just like learning new sports requires practice and exercise with the body. He was glad that students seemed to be developing an understanding that hard work and teamwork were keys to learning for all of them.

"And we learned last year that if we watch how someone does it, and then try it ourselves working with a partner or group, then pretty soon we'll be able to do it easily on our own. It's like a trick to make reading easier. So here's how I'd code the first paragraph." Jamie explained how he'd put a sticky note with an X near Columbus's birthplace—Genoa, Italy—and another note with an X next to the line that said, "Columbus first traveled to the Canary Islands." Then he showed them how he'd put a note with a check next to the line that said the voyage was filled with danger, especially because of pirates.

"I have a great book on pirates and I know that, even today, there are pirates robbing boats over near the Middle East and Africa." Mr. Yuan chimed in, "I'd put a note with a check on it where it says they were seeking a sea route to China, because my grandparents were Chinese and they have some old trade maps on the walls of their house."

"Now it's your turn," declared Bernard. "You read and code paragraphs 2 and 3, and Jamie and I will come around and help or answer your questions."

Mr. Yuan noticed almost everyone began to read—some silently, some in whispers to their partners. Bernard went over to Andrew, bringing him a book.

"You can put notes on the maps, too."

"On the map?" asked Andrew. "I thought we had to code what we read."

"Sure," said Bernard, "but last year Ms. Carson told us that you also have to read graphs and pictures 'cause there's a lot of info there that may not be written out in sentences." Jamie and Bernard walked around helping and nodding as they observed the other students. Students caught on quickly and worked together well. Mr. Yuan wanted Jamie and Bernard to do the reading as well.

"Great job, guys. Why don't you be partners and complete the coding on the reading. Once you finish coding the chapter, you can talk with one another about where your codes were the same and where they were different—and why."

Twenty minutes later most of the students were still reading and coding with the sticky notes, and Mr. Yuan noticed that two sets of partners were discussing their sticky notes together.

After Reading/Learning

"Fine job!" he complimented. "Okay, now I want each pair to Turn and Talk to another pair of students. Raise your hand every time you find a place where all four of you coded with an X and I will come over and we can talk about it." As the hands began to rise, he moved around the room to see what the common problems were. Vocabulary, he noted, and geographical places. As he listened and responded, Mr. Yuan realized that Coding helped him realize what the students did or didn't understand. This is good for the kids, and good for me, he thought.

"How did you like coding when you read?" Mr. Yuan asked the class.

"It was okay," said Danielle. "I think I understood more."

"I liked it," said Josh. "It made me slow down and pay more attention."

"I'm not sure," responded Renee, "It's kind of different."

"I wanted to know if Carly coded things the same as I did," said Annika.

"I didn't really like it because it made me have to read much slower than I usually do but I guess it made me think more," replied Sam.

"So I think we will do this again with the next chapter, but we will add another code: V for new vocabulary," said Mr. Yuan.

"For homework, make a list of the terms and places that you were not familiar with in the reading and write down what you think they mean now that we have talked about them. And think about whether there are other codes that would be worthwhile to use when reading. We can put them up on the board and vote on the ones the class wants to use. Good work today!"

PART 5: Expanding and Deepening Understanding after Reading/Learning

Introduction

We know that learning is a social activity, yet we often assign students to complete work in isolation. We also know that to expand and deepen learning, students need to transfer the new knowledge they have developed into new forms. That is, they need to write about it from a different point of view, put it into their own words, create pictures and graphical representations, and use specific protocols to talk about, rework, and communicate the content to others. Most students do not find reading and answering questions on their own to be motivating or helpful to their learning of content. In contrast, students report that when they work in groups, translate content into new formats, and apply understanding to new situations they typically find these activities helpful to their learning—and much more fun!

In Part 5 of the Toolkit, you will find a selection of student learning strategies, collaborative routines, and teacher instructional practices designed to help students consolidate their reading and learning. Note that this section of the Toolkit has many collaborative routines. Using these regularly in the classroom will promote higher engagement throughout the reading/learning process as they provide an authentic purpose for completing the work.

In this section of the Toolkit, you will find the following approaches to support reading and learning:

	Reading and Learning Phases		
	Before	**During**	**After**
Student Learning Strategies			
Role-Audience-Format-Topic (RAFT)	P	✓	✓
Sum It Up	P	✓	✓
Picture This!	P		✓
Collaborative Routines			
Save the Last Word for Me	P	✓	✓
Give One, Get One, Move On	P		✓
Jigsaw	P	✓	✓
Group Summarizing	P	✓	✓
Teacher Practices			
Problematic Situation	P	✓	✓
Classroom Scenarios			
Use of *Sum It Up* in an Elementary Mathematics Classroom	P	✓	✓
Use of *Save the Last Word for Me* in a Middle School English Classroom	P	✓	✓

Note: A **P** indicates that the strategy, routine, or practice helps students set a *purpose for reading* and a check mark indicates the focus of use.

Role-Audience-Format-Topic (RAFT)

Description

Role-Audience-Format-Topic (RAFT) asks students to creatively analyze and synthesize the information from a particular text or texts by taking on a specific role or perspective, defining the target audience, and choosing an appropriate written format to convey their understanding of the content topic (Santa, 1988; Vandervanter, in Adler, 1982).

Common Core Connection	Instructional Shift
A **Role-Audience-Format-Topic (RAFT)** learning activity helps students use what they learn from a text and communicate it from a specific point of view to a particular audience. This tool may be used as a performance task, offering students a choice to convey their understanding of Reading, Writing, Speaking & Listening, and Language standards. When using a RAFT as an assessment tool, be certain the choices of role, audience, format, and topic are standards based. Also be certain that the choices can be measured against a common rubric.	2, 3

Purpose

Use *before*, *during*, and *after* reading to

- Enhance comprehension of main ideas, organization, and point of view.

- Process information and reflect.

- Provide a creative approach for communicating what was learned that enhances engagement in writing or presentation tasks.

- Encourage students to consider perspectives different than their own.

- Help students communicate what they have learned using their preferred learning styles.

Directions

1. Explain what a **RAFT** is and why it is helpful.

2. Model a **RAFT** for students using a simple text or well-known concept or topic.

3. Assign a text for students to read. Before reading, note the different perspectives in the text.

4. Brainstorm three or four possible **RAFTs** students could choose.

5. Asks students to select **RAFTs** to communicate their learning.

RAFT Examples for a Unit on Exercise

Role	Audience	Format	Topic
Newspaper reporter	Readers in the United States	Feature	Health habits of U.S. regions
Lawyer	U.S. Supreme Court	Appeal speech	Right not to exercise
Inventor	Patent office	Petition	Revolutionary exercise machine
Heart	Person	Complaint	Not enough exercise
Boss	Employees	E-mail	Encouraging more exercise

Extensions

Have students work in cooperative pairs or small groups.

Have individual students or small groups brainstorm the four **RAFT** components rather than using the teacher-created list.

Have students present their **RAFT** writings or presentations to other audiences.

Role-Audience-Format-Topic (RAFT) Template

Name: _____

Date: _____

Concept to Be Addressed in the **RAFT** _____

Ideas for RAFTs Related to This Concept

Role	Audience	Format	Topic

© 2011 Public Consulting Group

Student's Choice for RAFT Components

Role _____

Audience _____

Format _____

Topic _____

Role-Audience-Format-Topic (RAFT) Content Examples

Mathematics

Have students demonstrate their understanding of geometrical concepts.

Role	Audience	Format	Topic
Architect	Editor of *Geometric Homes Journal*	Advertisement	Two- and three-dimensional shapes
Student group	School board	Cover letter and design for baseball field	Transformations and symmetry
Toy	Designer	Children's instructions for simple puzzles	Geometric shapes

Science

Have students summarize their understanding of the potential impact of earthquakes and volcanoes.

Role	Audience	Format	Topic
Research lab scientist	City planning board	Presentation on needed regulations	Probability of earthquake within 20 years
Doomsday religious fanatic	Protest at governor's office	Pamphlets and home videos	Recent volcano eruption in state is proof the end is near
Neighbors	Environmental Protection Agency (EPA)	Petition for insurance coverage	Need for EPA to require insurance for earthquake damage

Social Studies

Help students connect aspects of foreign cultures to their own lives using RAFTs.

Role	Audience	Format	Topic
Peace Corp volunteer	U.S. president	Letter and white paper	Increasing U.S. financial support to rural areas
Teacher	Foreign exchange students	Photo-journalism presentations	Literature reflects cultural history and values
Children	Alien from outer space	Discussion	Who they are

English Language Arts

Example of RAFT choices for an essay on genocide.

Role	Audience	Format	Topic
Citizen of Darfur	United Nations	Speech	Steps the United Nations and world nations can take to prevent genocide
Director of an anti-genocide organization	International Criminal Court (ICC)	Dialogue	How criminal tribunals like the ICC can contribute to genocide prevention
President Obama	U.S. Congress	Essay/Public Service Announcement	What the United States can do to stop genocide from occurring

Sum It Up

Description

Sum It Up requires readers to select important words that relate to the main ideas of a text selection and to use them in a one- or two-sentence summary (Reading Quest, 2015).

Common Core Connection	Instructional Shifts
Sum It Up is a starting point for helping students identify key ideas in a text and connect them to create a summary of the text (CCRA.R.2). By collaborating, students learn from one another. This strategy should be used as a jumping-off point for learning how to summarize, not an end goal.	1, 3

Purpose

Use *after* reading to

- Focus students' attention on key words in the reading and how to use them to develop a summary.

- Help students develop a process for selecting key words.

- Help students use critical thinking to make decisions about what words to include in order to create an effective summary.

- Provide an opportunity for students to make choices.

Directions

1. Have students read the entire text selection or a designated portion of a text and underline the key words and main ideas, or list them on paper.

2. Distribute the **Sum It Up** template. In pairs or small groups, ask students to share their lists and reach a consensus on what words are important. These main idea words should be listed on the **Sum It Up** template in the space provided.

3. Ask them to write a one- or two-sentence summary of the important ideas of the text, using as many of the main idea words as possible. Together, the sentence(s) may only contain 20 words. Note: Establish up front if articles and conjunctions (*and, the*) count as words.

4. When each group has completed this activity, ask the groups to write their summaries on chart paper or the interactive whiteboard. Compare their responses. If students read different portions of the same text, note that some of their sentences could now be put together to create a summary of the important ideas of the entire text.

Extensions

Have students create a summary sentence about what they know about the topic before reading the text. After they finish the **Sum It Up** activity, have them compare their knowledge before and after reading.

Have students complete **Sum It Ups** independently.

Have students **Sum It Up** in different numbers of words: 10, 15, and 25.

Sum It Up Template

Name: _____

Date: _____

Reading Selection: _____

1. List key words that convey the main ideas of the text.

2. When done, circle the key words that are most important about the text.

_____   _____

_____   _____

_____   _____

_____   _____

_____   _____

_____   _____

_____   _____

_____   _____

3. Using the words you circled, summarize the reading selection in one or two sentence(s), together containing only 20 words.

_____ _____ _____ _____

_____ _____ _____ _____

_____ _____ _____ _____

_____ _____ _____ _____

_____ _____ _____ _____

Sum It Up Content Examples

Mathematics

Elementary School

In the Everyday Math program, fifth-grade students have an integrated portion in each unit called the American Tour. As students read the section, have them use the **Sum It Up** strategy to help them focus on important words related to the main idea and then use these words in a one- or two-sentence summary. This collaborative routine will promote higher engagement as students read in math class to gain information to solve problems.

Middle School

As students read through the section of the text about circle graphs, have them list key words from the section on a piece of paper. Instruct students to work in pairs or small groups to share and discuss their lists of key words. Direct students to discuss the importance of their word lists to the main idea of the section. Ask students to write a summary of which data are most appropriate to be represented in a circle graph and why.

High School

After students read a section in their algebra books on exponential growth and exponential decay, have them use the **Sum It Up** template to explain a key concept in the text.

Science

Elementary School

To engage upper elementary students in a new science unit about microorganisms, have them read an account from a book or a website about medical mysteries, in which scientists are depicted racing against time to determine the cause and cure for a newly discovered disease. An interesting example is the discovery of Lyme disease, which is caused by a single-celled bacterium that's transmitted by deer tick larvae. Have students work in pairs and use the **Sum It Up** strategy to focus on the key ideas about microorganisms and disease in the story or article they read.

Middle School

While studying about temperature and density, students can read a good summary article or research the Internet to find information about various real-world situations in which thermal energy is transferred by means of currents. Examples include convection cells within an enclosed room, in the atmosphere, in the ocean, and under the Earth. Model the **Sum It Up** strategy with one article, and then have students use the strategy with the other readings they encounter.

High School

An applied physics curriculum should include links from core science concepts to technological applications in the real world. Assign pairs of students to read different chapters in the book *To Engineer Is Human: The Role of Failure in Successful Design* as a way of demonstrating how engineers use knowledge of science and technology to solve practical problems. Ask student pairs to use the **Sum It Up** strategy to help them develop an effective summary that can be shared in **Jigsaw** fashion with the rest of the class.

Social Studies

Elementary School

After reading a textbook section on the geography of South America, have students complete **Sum It Up** to create statements about different countries and about the continent as a whole. Have students compare the summary statements completed at different levels of detail to develop an understanding of how summarizing changes with the topic.

Middle School

After reading a series of letters sent by soldiers during the Civil War, have students use **Sum It Up** to write increasingly brief summaries of what they learned about life during this time. Have students write one sentence using 20 words. Then, have students eliminate five words and rewrite the sentence. Compare these sentences and engage students in a discussion about what they kept and what they eliminated.

High School

After reading about and listening to a collection of important presidential speeches, use **Sum It Up** both as a way to have students distill the key messages in the speeches and also to synthesize information across speeches to determine how key themes have stayed the same and have changed over time.

English Language Arts

Elementary School

After reading a picture book as a class, use **Sum It Up** to develop early facility with summarizing. Review each page, asking students to identify the important words. Collect these as a class. Have students vote on whether each word is one of the most important to the text. Finally, have students work in pairs to write a sentence or two that summarizes the book. Share these summaries with the class.

Middle School

During the reading of a whole-class novel, use **Sum It Up** at the ends of chapters as a way for students to review the events. Have students work in pairs to list key words, circle the most important ones, and construct their 20-word summaries. Then, at the end of the novel, provide each of these summaries to students and have them develop a collection of summaries they think best summarizes the novel.

High School

During and *after* reading, use **Sum It Up** to help students summarize complex pieces of writing efficiently. Provide students with practice using this strategy with a wide variety of genres. Have students think aloud the different strategies they use to summarize longer versus shorter texts.

Picture This!

Description

Picture This! is an after-reading comprehension-building strategy that helps readers apply higher-order thinking skills to their experiences as readers. The strategy asks students to visually represent three to six key scenes or points from a fiction or nonfiction text supported by related captions and text quotes for each picture. It is a versatile strategy that can be adapted for many types of reading assignments and content areas.

Common Core Connection	Instructional Shift
Be certain that **Picture This!** addresses your learning target standards. The merit of a particular series of drawings should be, taken together, how well they summarize the text and how well evidence is deployed in explaining the choices (CCRA.R.1-3). Artistic ability should not be a grading criteria.	2

Purpose

Use *after* reading to

- Translate ideas from text to image.

- Evaluate, summarize, and present evidence or support from the text.

- Assess reading comprehension.

Directions

1. After reading a short piece of text together, choose with the class three main points from the story or nonfiction selection. Discuss how each might be represented visually, how each might be captioned, and which quotes from the text best accompany each image. Discuss how the **Picture This!** strategy is another way to create a summary.

2. After reading a novel or a longer nonfiction work, ask students (individually, in pairs, or in groups of four or five) to select the three to six most crucial turning points of the novel or critical pieces of information from the nonfiction work. These can be broadly or narrowly defined, depending on the assessment goals for the unit.

3. Ask students to create pictures, diagrams, or images connected to the text. Students should convey details expressed in the text in their visual representations.

4. For each picture, students should write a caption explaining what the image depicts. This should be a one- to two-sentence summary statement of the ideas and importance of each image.

5. For each picture, students should select and copy a passage from the text connected to the image's importance in some way. Again, the requirement for the selection of the text will vary according to the assessment goals for the unit.

Extensions

Use **Picture This!** when all students read the same text or when students in pairs or groups read different texts related to the same unit of study.

Ask students to defend their choices of key events and map students' selections to determine what students saw as most important.

Use **Picture This!** as a scaffold for analytical writing about a text.

Use **Picture This!** as an assessment strategy when students are reading multiple texts.

Use **Picture This!** as a presentation strategy for **Jigsaw** groups when different texts are read about the same topic.

Have students take on the role of a text character, author, or personified object when completing the **Picture This!** assignment so that they understand how point of view impacts mental Imagery.

Picture This! Template

Name: _____

Date: _____

Reading Selection: _____

Directions

Choose important parts of the text selection related to the learning target or prompt and picture them in your mind. Draw three to six pictures in the boxes that match your mental image. Give each picture a caption and write a quote from the text that relates to it.

Caption _____ **Quote** _____	**Caption** _____ **Quote** _____
Caption _____ **Quote** _____	**Caption** _____ **Quote** _____
Caption _____ **Quote** _____	**Caption** _____ **Quote** _____

Picture This! Content Examples

English Language Arts

During a study of metaphor and simile.

Have students identify these in a text (CCRA.R.4) and use **Picture This!** to capture the quote and illustrate the simile.

Caption: The attackers were like this eagle, fierce, quick, and merciless.

Quote: "The attackers struck like eagles, crook-clawed, hook-beaked, swooping down from a mountain ridge to harry smaller birds." (from *The Odyssey*)

Mathematics

After an elementary school lesson or textbook chapter on large numbers.

Have students identify several comparisons for large numbers and create pictures for those representations.

Caption: A million dollars would be about as long as this football field.

Quote: "One million dollar bills stacked would be roughly 333 feet tall."

Science

During a middle school science unit about sound.

Students investigate a variety of noise-making objects and musical instruments, ultimately determining that all things that make sound cause the air to vibrate in some way. After reading about different musical instruments from around the world, have students use the **Picture This!** template to figure out and then illustrate the special way(s) that each instrument causes the air to vibrate in order to produce sound.

Caption: When the musician blows air, his lips vibrate and the air in the didgeridoo vibrates, too.

Quote: "The didgeridoo is played with continuously vibrating lips to produce the drone."

Social Studies

During the reading of a textbook section on the different structures in local and state government.

Have students use **Picture This!** to describe each function and explain something significant about each.

Caption: The scales illustrate that the judicial branch deals with justice and with making sure that the laws legislators pass are in line with the Constitution.

Quote: "The Supreme Court serves as an important check on the power of the other branches through its power to decide whether laws uphold or violate the principles laid out in the Constitution."

Save the Last Word for Me

Description

Save the Last Word for Me is a small-group discussion protocol that supports collaborative discussion of a text (developed by Daniel Baron and Patricia Averette).

Common Core Connection	Instructional Shifts
Students stay focused and motivated when they have a specific purpose for reading a text in order to complete a task. Make **Save the Last Word for Me** an evidence-based activity. Students' reasons for choosing a quote should be justified from within the text or topic. Students should not be able to say, "Because I liked it," or "It reminds me of . . . " They can certainly choose a quote because they have an opinion on it. Modeling this in a small-group Fishbowl discussion would help students understand teacher expectations.	1, 2

Purpose

Use *during* and *after* reading to

- Support students' interaction with text.
- Promote reading comprehension.
- Clarify and deepen thinking about content.

Directions

1. Divide students into groups of three to five. Give each student three index cards or the **Save the Last Word for Me** template.

2. Assign a text selection to read. Ask students to write quotations they find interesting on one side of the card and why they find each quote interesting on the opposite side of the card, or use the template to record.

3. After everyone is finished reading the selection and choosing quotes, the first person in each group shares one of his or her quotes but does not say why this interested him or her.

4. After everyone has taken about 1 minute to react or respond to the shared quote, the person who chose the quote shares why he or she selected it.

5. Discussion continues in this fashion with each person in the group taking one to three turns as time permits.

Extensions

Have the group complete a group summary of the text that was read.

Have the group debrief the session.

Have each person select a quote to write about in a response journal.

Ask each group to select the most important quote to share with the class with justification about why it was seen as significant.

Save the Last Word for Me Template

Name: _____

Date: _____

Reading Selection: _____

Directions

Fill in the following three boxes with quotes that strike you as particularly interesting from the text. Make sure to copy the quote accurately and note the page where the quote is found. Then, below each quote, write why the quote interested you or what it made you think about. Bring the completed template to the meeting with your small group.

First Quote

Page #____

Reason for selecting this quote

Second Quote

Page #____

Reason for selecting this quote

Third Quote

Page #____

Reason for selecting this quote

Save the Last Word for Me Content Examples

English Language Arts

After reading a poetry unit

Have students copy a stanza from a poem onto a card in which they find the language particularly fresh, engaging, or beautiful. On the reverse side of the card, ask students to analyze the impact of the poet's specific word choices on meaning and tone, such as:

Archibald MacLeish, *Eleven*

"And summer mornings the mute child, rebellious, / Stupid, hating the words, the meanings, hating / The Think now, Think, the O but Think! Would leave / On tiptoe"—MacLeish's use of cadence and repetition ("hating the words, the meanings, hating / The Think now") emphasizes the narrator's frustration with the restriction he feels and his desire to "leave / On tiptoe" and be free.

Robert Frost, *Birches*

"But swinging doesn't bend them down to stay / As ice storms do."—Frost contrasts the ephemeral, imaginative quality of human action on the trees ("swinging") with the objective truth of the natural world ("ice storms").

Mathematics

Before, during, and *after* reading the calculus j-operator unit on imaginary number properties

"The imaginary unit is denoted by the symbol j."—Because my name is Jay and I love science fiction and its imaginary inventions and machines.

"It is impossible to square any real number and have the product equal a negative number. We must define a new number system if we wish to include square roots of negative numbers."—That always made me curious when we worked with square roots before now.

"We need merely to multiply numerator and denominator by the conjugate of the denominator in order to perform this operation."—It's just so funny that the author keeps using adjectives like "merely" to show how easy calculus is and after 10 weeks in this course, I still have trouble understanding this book.

Science

During and *after* reading newspaper articles about current science issues

"Fluorescent filaments of the organisms, known as cyanobacteria, began forming in the river last week and by yesterday they streaked the Esplanade lagoons a psychedelic green."—A tiny bacteria caused a major transformation in a short period of time and I wonder how they will get the algae under control.

"Carnoustie, Scotland—Rain was pelting. Sideways, as they say over here. It was a cold rain, too. And the wind? Surely, even the foundation of Glamis Castle had to be shaking."—I picked this as the only part of the paper I really like reading is the sports section and I enjoy learning how weather affects sports, in this case golf.

Social Studies

During and *after* reading the U.S. Constitution, Articles, and Amendments

"We the people of the United States, in order to form a more perfect Union, establish justice, insure domestic tranquility, provide for the common defense, promote the general welfare, and secure the blessings of liberty to ourselves and our posterity."—Because it says it all and because I'm worried we're losing ground in achieving this vision.

"The right of citizens of the United States, who are eighteen years of age or older, to vote shall not be denied or abridged by the United States or any state on account of age."—I'll be 18 next year and only at the very end in Amendment 26 is it reflected that youth's ideas are important.

Give One, Get One, Move On

Description

Give One, Get One, Move On supports collaborative reflection on, interaction with, or review of a reading selection by using a protocol to solicit responses from multiple readers.

Common Core Connection	Instructional Shifts
Give One, Get One, Move On works best as an after-reading activity. While students might think they know something about a topic, it's not a good idea to reinforce what might be an incorrect piece of information by sharing it widely. This strategy is a great way to get students moving, reinforce learning, and prepare for writing or another assessment. The teacher can circulate to listen and evaluate what students are saying. If there are too many misconceptions, the teacher may decide to reteach.	1, 3

Purpose

Use *before* reading to

- Help students brainstorm key ideas on a topic or reading to activate prior knowledge and build background knowledge.

Use *after* reading to

- Help students to summarize and synthesize key concepts in the reading.

Directions

1. Set up a box matrix with six or nine boxes and hand out copies.

2. Ask students to write the topic of the template in the "Topic" section. Then ask them to think of an important idea about the topic and write it in the first box.

3. Set up a rotation pattern (for example, pass to the left) by instructing students to pass the sheet to another student.

4. Students read what was written in the first box and write an idea in box 2. It can be the same idea they put in box 1 on their own sheets, as long as it is not the same idea that appears on the sheet that was passed to them. No ideas can be repeated on a paper. If the student's idea already appears on the paper, he or she has to think of another idea to write.

5. Students continue passing on each paper, reading the ideas, and adding new ideas until all of the boxes are filled with ideas.

6. Each sheet is returned to the original owner to read and reflect on.

Extensions

Use **Give One, Get One, Move On** as a summary of different text around the same topic.

Set up a template to reflect different points of view or different arguments.

Have students write summaries based on the sheets that they get back.

Use **Give One, Get One, Move On** to generate ways to respond to a text, story ideas for writing, and the like.

Use **Give One, Get One, Move On** to help students summarize or reflect on a lecture or presentation.

Give One, Get One, Move On Template

Name: _____

Date: _____

Directions

Write the topic in the first section. Think of an important idea you have learned today. Write it down in box 1. Pass the sheet to another student who will read silently what was written in the first box. That student will add an idea in box 2. Do not repeat ideas that are already listed. Continue passing on the paper and adding ideas until all of the boxes are filled with ideas. Return the sheet to the original owner.

Topic		
1	2	3
4	5	6
7	8	9

Developed by Roz Weizer. Used with permission.

© 2011 Public Consulting Group

Give One, Get One, Move On Content Examples

Mathematics

Elementary School

After a unit on polygons, pass out a **Give One, Get One, Move On** template, with nine boxes, to each student. Have students write "Polygons" in the topic box. Explain to students that the reason for this activity is to help them remember what they learned during this unit. Ask students to think of an important fact they remember about polygons and record it in the first box. Have students complete the Give One, Get One, Move On activity and ask students to pass their templates. Remind students that no idea can be repeated. When the templates make their way back to the original students, have them read over the sheets and write a short explanation of the important facts about polygons from their templates.

Middle School

To help students summarize the key concepts taught in an integrated math program, use the **Give One, Get One, Move On** template after each module. Set up a box matrix of six to nine boxes on a sheet of paper. Inform students that they will be passing the sheet of paper around to one another to record important concepts they have been studying during the module.

Topic: Health and Fitness

Studying sleep data	Using circle graphs	Using line graphs to record calories burned while swimming
Finding heart rate	Understanding capacity	Reading graphs (box and whisker)
Finding volume	Percents	Slope of a line

When every box on the matrix is filled, have students read over their sheets to remember the important concepts and reflect on how the concepts are connected to the module theme.

High School

Before students read the section in their geometry books on geometric probability and area of sectors, have them use the **Give One, Get One, Move On** template to brainstorm what they remember about probability. This strategy will support collaborative reflection and help students review what they have learned in past math classes around probability. This will allow students to activate prior knowledge needed to connect to the new learning of probability and geometric measure.

Science

Elementary School

After reading a textbook section on forest habitats, gauge students' understanding of survival needs and habitats by giving them a **Give One, Get One, Move On** template with the recorded topic: "Ways organisms use a pine tree as part of their habitats." Different students should be able to add representative examples, such as animals using the pine seeds for food, or birds using tree cavities for a nesting shelter, or others using the water that collects on the branches.

Middle School

After reading an article or textbook section on different forms of energy, use this strategy to have students consider the types of energy that are at play in different toys and the energy transformations that make the toys function. Create flow charts to show the transfer and transformation of energy that is happening in each toy and then have students choose one toy to write about, describing the toy, and explaining the energy transformations (including loss of energy to heat). Have students use a **Give One, Get One, Move On** template to help them synthesize what they've learned about energy transformations.

High School

Explore the unifying concept of plate tectonics through reading and hand-on explorations such as map observations (to see the matching shapes of the continents) and demonstrations of the actions that take place at the boundaries between different plates, then read historical accounts of the developing evidence of the mechanisms that explain the movement of continents. Provide students with a **Give One, Get One, Move On** template after reading about all of the lines of evidence, and ask them to fill in the boxes with the different ideas that converged to support this theory.

Social Studies

Elementary School

After learning about the different necessary parts of a community, use **Give One, Get One, Move On** as a way for students to review all of those structures. Use the template as a springboard for extension activities, such as having students describe how the structures are connected or to consider what would happen to a community if one of the structures—such as the fire department—were eliminated.

Middle School

Use this collaborative routine as a way to help students review the responsibilities of a citizen in a democracy. **Give One, Get One, Move On** might be used either to have students list different examples of a specific responsibility—voting—or to consider and rank several broad areas of responsibility.

High School

After a unit on World War II, use **Give One, Get One, Move On** to have students review the factors that led to the war. Once the templates have all been completed, list the factors on the board or digital display and rank them according to the number of students who have them on their graphic organizers. Then, identify missing factors and ask students to discuss which factors were, according to their learning, the most important and why. Use this as a way to develop students' capacity to synthesize important information.

English Language Arts

Elementary and Middle School

Note:

This strategy is text-agnostic and so was not differentiated for elementary and middle school.

Provide a brief, grade-appropriate common text to small reading groups, and ask students to independently read and annotate the text. Once they have finished, ask students to choose one of their best annotations and record it on the **Give One, Get One, Move On** template. Once the templates are completed, engage students in a small-group or whole-class discussion to see what other students' annotations added to their understanding of the text.

High School

During and *after* reading a novel with substantial symbolism, use **Give One, Get One, Move On** both between sections of a text and after reading to help students synthesize information about symbolism and figurative language. These activities can be collected by students and used for review at the end of the novel.

Jigsaw

Description

Jigsaw is a group-learning strategy in which students read different portions of a text and then share what they have learned with the small group. It effectively involves all students in a learning task and provides opportunity for differentiated learning (Aronson, Blaney, Stephin, Sikes, & Snapp, 1978).

Common Core Connection	Instructional Shifts
Jigsaw is a time-honored collaborative strategy that remains a winner in the era of college and career-ready standards. It breaks long, complex text into manageable chunks and ensures that all students will know and be able to teach others their chunks of information, regardless of their own reading ability. Teachers can structure the Jigsaw groups to support particular students. Caution: Jigsaw can only be done with text in which each chunk is a discrete concept. That is, a chunk given to one group can't be dependent on knowing the information from the chunk that came before it.	1, 3

Purpose

Use *during* and *after* reading to

- Involve students in reading and communicating what they have learned with their peers.

- Address a wide range of student abilities and interests using reading tasks of differing reading levels, genres, text lengths, and topics.

- Connect different types of reading materials linked to a common theme.

- Help students develop reading, listening, and speaking skills and learn from others how to construct and convey important concepts from written text.

- Engage students through small-group interactions.

- Develop understanding about a topic without having every student read every reading selection.

- Provide practice in synthesizing information from text and communicating that information to others.

Directions

1. Identify what students need to learn from a unit of study and locate three to six reading selections that contain the desired content information. To avoid confusion during grouping, mark each selection with a number or color code. (Or select a single text that can be broken into several fairly even parts. This does not work well with texts that must be read sequentially, for which understanding one selection is dependent on having read the others.)

2. Organize students into small, differentiated groups of three to six members, depending on the number of reading selections.

3. Ask members of the small group to choose one reading selection each. Students will be responsible for reading and then communicating the information they learn to their small groups.

4. Explain the **Jigsaw** process to the whole class.

5. Reorganize students, grouping together those who will read the same selection into "Expert Teams."

6. Provide time for each student to read the selection and take notes or create a graphic organizer that identifies the important concepts and supporting details from their reading.

7. In their Expert Teams, members discuss what they have learned and plan how team members will share the information with their small groups.

8. Each "expert" returns to the original small group to explain the key concepts of the reading selection to the group members who did not read that selection.

9. In the small group, continue the sharing process until all experts have had a chance to share what they learned and to learn about and note the important ideas in all of the other reading selections.

Extensions

Use the **Jigsaw** for independent inquiry topics within a general unit of study.

Have each small group form three or four essential questions to be used for post-assessment of the learning.

Jigsaw Template

Name: _____

Date: _____

Topic: _____

Reading Selections Used in the Jigsaw

1. _____

2. _____

3. _____

4. _____
_____

Notes about selection # _____
_____
_____

Additional notes from other students who also read selection # _____
_____
_____

Student notes about selections not read
_____

_____
_____

_____
_____

_____
_____

_____

Jigsaw Content Examples

English Language Arts

After small-group reading of four novels on the theme of courage, using Literature Circle discussions

After Literature Circle discussions on the following topics, form **Jigsaw** groups, with one representative for each novel, to compare and contrast:

- The author's point of view about courage
- Examples of courageous actions of characters
- The plot problem, crisis, and denouement about courage
- Examples of how figurative language, symbols, and other literary devices were used to develop the theme of courage

Mathematics

Before beginning a unit on functions

Activate prior knowledge by having four small groups of students discuss what they already know about functions, then break into **Jigsaw** groups for students to lead the review of different definitions, practical applications, and ways of understanding functions with their peers, such as:

- Input/output machines
- Ways of describing one quantity determining another
- Application: interest rates/return on investment
- Domain and range
- Mathematical expressions

Science

During and *after* reading text and online materials about the cardiovascular system

Form study groups to collaboratively read and research one of the three following areas, then form **Jigsaw** groups after reading is completed for peers to share materials and teach one another the essential components and related vocabulary for each system:

- Blood composition
- The heart
- Vessels and blood circulation

Social Studies

During and *after* reading about the early Roman world and the expansion of Rome

Have students self-select from the following topics for small-group research, followed by **Jigsaw** presentations that include information, visual depictions, and links to today's world:

- The arts of government
- Roman life and society
- Roman art and architecture
- Cicero and Rome
- Virgil's poetry

Group Summarizing

Description

Group Summarizing supports students to work together to preview text before reading, locate supporting information and examples during reading, summarize their ideas on a four-quadrant chart after reading, and use the notes to scaffold the writing of a group or individual summary.

Common Core Connection	Instructional Shifts
Group Summarizing would be a good next step after students have tried **Sum It Up**. The skill of summary is very difficult for some students to learn because it requires both a deep understanding of the text and an ability to manipulate and condense language. Working collaboratively, students support and learn from one another. The teacher can scaffold for students by gradually reducing the number of topics he or she provides until students are coming up with them on their own.	1, 3

Purpose

Use *during* and *after* reading to

- Involve students in constructing a meaningful synthesis of what they have read.

- Help students learn how to do a summary before they are asked to create their own.

- Provide practice in paraphrasing.

- Allow students to demonstrate understanding of concepts through the completed group summary chart.

- Link the different parts of the reading process.

- Develop higher-order critical thinking skills.

Directions

1. Model the group summary process by preparing an example of a completed chart.

2. Divide students into small groups.

3. Have each student create a four-quadrant chart and label each quadrant with the appropriate topic or concept. Explain that the purpose for reading is to learn important information about each of the topics or concepts they selected.

4. During reading, students jot down notes under each heading with page number references.

5. After students have read the text and made their notes, instruct the group to discuss with one another what information and ideas they found that were important about the key words or concepts on the chart.

---

6. When the group agrees that the supporting information is important, it is added to the chart.

7. Once the charts are finished, ask the group to reread what they have written and be sure their ideas are clearly expressed.

8. Then have the group collaboratively put the ideas together in a written summary, typically one to three paragraphs, on chart paper so that they can share their summaries with other groups.

Extensions

Ask students to preview the text passage or chapter before reading to identify four major topics or concepts presented by the text author.

Have students create their charts on an interactive whiteboard or wall poster so that others in the class can see how the ideas of other groups are similar or different.

Have students use the group summary chart to write individual summaries.

Group Summarizing Template

Name: _____

Date: _____

Reading Selection: _____

Directions

1. As you read, take notes on your Individual Summary Chart about important information related to the four key topics or ideas. List the paragraph or page numbers next to each note.

2. Form small groups to discuss your ideas and come to agreement on important information that should be listed in each of the four key topic/idea quadrants. Add the agreed-upon ideas to the Group Summary Chart. Reread the final chart to be sure all ideas have been clearly expressed.

3. Collaboratively write a group summary, typically one to three paragraphs. When you have finished, copy it onto a large sheet of chart paper so that it can be shared with other groups.

Individual Summary Chart

Key Topic/Idea	Key Topic/Idea
Key Topic/Idea	Key Topic/Idea

© 2011 Public Consulting Group

Group Summary Chart

Key Topic/Idea	Key Topic/Idea
Key Topic/Idea	Key Topic/Idea

Important!

On separate paper, collaboratively write a summary of one to three paragraphs using the group notes. When the group has reviewed and agreed on the summary, copy it onto large chart paper so that it can be shared with other groups.

Group Summarizing Content Examples

English Language Arts	Mathematics
After reading a complex novel or short story, such as *St. Lucy's Home for Girls Raised by Wolves*	*During* and *after* reading a chapter on points, lines, planes, and angles
Formulate four statements for students to respond to in the Individual Summary Chart, then work in groups to agree on summary points based on the novel for the Group Summary Chart, such as:	Replace teacher front-loading with **Group Summarizing**. Possible postulates to summarize:

English Language Arts:

- Acclimating to a new culture versus preserving one's identity
- Peer influence
- The pros and cons of socialization and becoming "civilized"
- The author's use of the girls as werewolves to describe a universal human condition

Mathematics:

- Ruler postulate
- Segment addition postulate
- Protractor postulate
- Angle addition postulate

Science	Social Studies
During and *after* reading, watching demonstrations, and solving related problems about electrostatics	*During* and *after* reading several civics text chapters about the functions of government
Use **Group Summarizing** to review primary concepts for the unit test, such as:	Widen students' perspectives about government by having them individually take notes and then check their understanding with their peers about:

Science:

- Conservation of charge
- Coulomb's law
- Charging by friction and contact
- Charging by induction

Social Studies:

- Laws and rules
- Distributed, shared, and limited powers
- Organization and relationships of national, state, and local governments
- Operations of the U.S. government under the Constitution

Problematic Situation

Description

Problematic Situation is a strategy whereby teachers introduce a compelling problem or scenario that establishes a purpose for reading to engage student interest and stimulate inquiry (Vacca & Vacca, 1993).

Common Core Connection	Instructional Shifts
Turn **Problematic Situation** on its head to serve as both a purpose for reading and a performance task after reading.	1, 3

Purpose

Use *during* and *after* reading to

- Engage students.

- Make connections to new concepts.

- Focus readers on the main ideas presented in text.

- Help readers analyze problem/solution relationships.

- Ask students to provide supporting evidence.

Directions

1. Design a motivating **Problematic Situation** to stimulate students' interest about important information or concepts in the text material they will read. The situation should be authentic and require analytical or evaluative thinking to resolve. As appropriate, include affective components (for example, emotions, values) in the "problem."

2. Prior to asking students to read one or more text selections, introduce the **Problematic Situation** and, in cooperative groups, ask them to brainstorm possible results or solutions to the problem. Suggest that each group record their responses and discuss the pros and cons of each solution. Have the groups share their thinking with the whole class.

3. Ask students to read the text selection(s), looking for information that supports their solutions.

4. Ask students to refine or modify their initial solutions as they gain information and evidence from their reading.

5. Ask each group to share their solutions and explain the rationale for their decisions.

Extensions

Have students locate and use additional sources of information to support solutions.

Ask students to consider whether some of their own solutions might be preferable to the one presented by the author.

Use notes and responses as the basis for an analytical or persuasive essay.

Problematic Situation Content Examples

English Language Arts

Assignment: Read *One Flew Over the Cuckoo's Nest* by Robert Faggen

The school board has decided to ban this book due to its controversial language and content. Because the high school principal believes the book is valuable, she persuaded the school board to take public comments before making its final decision. Because this book is part of our curriculum, the principal has asked you to develop a presentation in support of the text. In order for you to be taken seriously, your presentation must acknowledge the controversial nature of the book as well as the reasons some may think it is inappropriate. What resources and other experts should you reference to persuade the school board? What in this book makes it valuable for people to read? How can you present this information and make a well-reasoned argument that the book is worth preserving in the school's curriculum?

Math

Assignment: Chapter on two- and three-dimensional geometric shapes

You have a new part-time job after school at a local architecture firm. Your boss is trying to help you see why math is an important part of architectural design. He shows you the designs for four new homes and asks you to find all of the geometric shapes in the designs and tells you that, by the end of the week, you need to find eight geometric shapes and tell him the name of each shape, describe it, and predict why that shape was chosen over other shapes for that house. Then you are to redesign one part of a house using a different geometric shape and explain why it's a better design for that house.

Science

Assignment: Energy article, www.eia.doe.gov/kids/energyfacts/sources/renewable/renewable.html

A company called Northeast Energy recognizes the limited supply of fossil fuels and they have been encouraging their clients to conserve energy. While conservation is an important step, at some point in the not-so-distant future, they realize our supplies of fossil fuels will be depleted and they will be forced to rely completely on alternative energy sources. You have been contracted to evaluate the feasibility of using perpetual and renewable energy sources to provide power for their clients, particularly solar, wind, hydroelectric, geothermal, biomass, and nuclear power. They are also interested in any other alternatives to fossil fuels of which you might be aware. What information can you provide that will help them in their future planning?

Social Studies

Assignment: Read chapter 7, "Ratifying the Constitution"

As a newspaper reporter in the late 1780s, you have been asked to write an editorial determining if the process established for ratifying the Constitution is fair. The publisher also wants you to discuss whether or not the Constitution should be ratified. Based on your knowledge of that time period, what arguments would you include in your editorial?

Use of *Sum It Up* in an Elementary Mathematics Classroom

Students in Mr. Morrison's class often use their fifth-grade *Student Reference Book* to find additional information about the mathematics they are learning. Today, Mr. Morrison has planned for students to read a selection that will inform them about the U.S. Decennial Census. Students will use this information as they study how and why census data is collected and demographic trends in the United States.

Before Reading/Learning

Mr. Morrison writes the word *census* on the board. "Michael, can you read the word on the board?"

Michael replies, "Census."

Mr. Morrison then asks the class, "Does this word sound familiar to anyone?" As he looks out at students' puzzled faces, Mr. Morrison asks students to turn to page 299 in the *Student Reference Book*. "We are about to start a new unit using a specific type of data, census data, collected as far back as 1790. Census data tells us how many people live in the United States. I would like you all to read this page in your reference book silently. As you read, I would like you to write down any key words and important facts or main ideas we should know and talk about to better understand how and why the United States does a census. Make sure you look at all parts of the page. Once you all have had a chance to read by yourself you will work with a partner and share."

During Reading/Learning

Mr. Morrison circulates and observes as students read and write. Some students finish quickly. "Did you read the notes section and the T graph section?" The students go back and read the sections they missed. "Who needs more time? Are you ready to work with your partners?" Almost all of the students give a thumbs-up.

"Before you start your work, I need to review with you the **Sum It Up** template. If you are not already sitting next to your work partner, move now."

While students are getting situated, Mr. Morrison passes out one copy of the **Sum It Up** template to each pair. "Please look up here at the screen. You all have received a copy of Sum It Up. I want you first to write the title of the reading selection we just read." Mr. Morrison points to where it says "Reading Selection" on the template being projected on the screen, "Right here. Now, as you share with your partner the key words you have identified, I want you to discuss and agree on which are the most important words to understand the main idea about the U.S. Census. You will then record these key words here." Mr. Morrison points to the first section on the Sum It Up template. "After you have recorded your list of words, write a one- or two-sentence summary of the important ideas from what you have read. Try to use as many as of the key words from the list generated. But try to keep your summary to a maximum of twenty words. Does this make sense? Are there any questions?"

Brian raises his hand and asks, "Do short words like *a* and *the* count as part of the twenty words?"

"What do you think, class? Should we count articles or conjunctions?"

"Yes," says Brian. His partner Reya nods.

"No, twenty words are not that many to write," replied Jim. Others seem to agree.

"Okay," said Mr. Morrison, "Let's not use articles or conjunctions as part of the word count. You can get started."

As Mr. Morrison moves around the room listening to students share their lists of key words, he is pleased with their discussions. Some students need assistance to get started with their summaries. Mr. Morrison reminds students of the three questions within the article. "If you think about how to answer these questions it should be very helpful as you write your summaries."

After Reading/Learning

"I have put three pieces of chart paper up on the wall around the room. Once you have finished your summaries, I want you to rewrite them on one of the pieces of chart paper." As students finish their summaries, they record them on the chart paper. Once the summaries are all up on the chart paper, Mr. Morrison asks students to do a carousel around the room to read each pair's summaries. Students move around the room discussing the summaries and what other students wrote compared with what they wrote. Collectively, the students show a working understanding of what a census is and how and why it is done.

"Now that you know what a census is and why it is done, we are going to start looking closer at the data collected. We will be looking at the types of questions that have been asked over the years and how they have changed. Does any one have any idea why the census would ask a question about telephones?" Some students start buzzing and others just laughed. The question seems to spark their interest in looking at census data. Mr. Morrison informs students that it is time for lunch and thinks how this is always a fun unit to teach. But he had not tried using the **Sum It Up** strategy before. It worked well, though, so he is thinking that he will use it again.

Use of *Save the Last Word for Me* in a Middle School English Classroom

Ms. Snow wondered how she could get her students to engage with poetry. She had read *Abandoned Farmhouse* last April during Poetry Month and thought it might be intriguing to some of the reluctant students as it was short in length, used ordinary language, and had a puzzling ending. She thought it would be a good way to introduce the unit on poetry. She considered initially focusing on visualization and how poets use language to create powerful lines, but she wanted to get students talking about the poem. She decided to try **Save the Last Word for Me**, a collaborative discussion strategy another teacher had mentioned.

Before Reading/Learning

Ms. Snow wrote the words *abandoned farmhouse* on the board. She asked students to close their eyes and for thirty seconds form a picture in their minds of an abandoned farmhouse. "Remember to use sensory details to make the image more vivid. What do you see, hear, smell, feel, and taste?" She paused in silence. "Keep that image and find a word that describes the abandoned farmhouse you visualized. We'll do a silent Chalk Talk. For the next two or three minutes, when you see a free piece of chalk, you can go up to the board and write your word. If your word relates to one that has already been written, draw a line that connects them." Students took turns filling the board with words. Afterwards, Ms. Snow asked students to note words they particularly liked and to determine why these words provoked a positive response. Then she solicited student ideas as to what a poem titled "Abandoned Farmhouse" might be about.

Ms. Snow divided a piece of chart paper into four sections and wrote one of these terms in each section: figurative language, imagery, symbolism, and tone. She explained that these words represent techniques poets use to create images in the reader's mind or to prompt feelings in the reader. She asked students if the terms were familiar to them. Several hands went up. "Great. But several of you are not raising your hands and I want to make sure you all know these. So, form a group of three and talk about each of the words and come up with an example. Then have someone in your group come write each of your examples under the correct term on the piece of chart paper. That way we will have a chart for you to refer to throughout the poetry unit. Let's take just seven minutes to get some examples up." Students pulled chairs together and discussed examples. There was a lively buzz in the room. Ms. Snow was impressed by the examples that were posted and felt they were a good resource for those who may struggle with the reading.

During Reading/Learning

Ms. Snow projected the first four lines of the poem on the wall. She informed the class that Ted Kooser served as poet laureate for the United States, which is the highest national honor for a living poet. She went on to read the first four lines aloud to the class:

Abandoned Farmhouse by Ted Kooser

He was a big man, says the size of his shoes
on a pile of broken dishes by the house;
a tall man too, says the length of the bed
in an upstairs room; and a good, God-fearing man,

Ms. Snow did a **Think-Aloud** to show the class how she read the poem, "Hmmm, I 'see' a big man with big feet and he has talking shoes. Now I am pretty sure that no one has invented talking shoes, so the poet is giving the shoes human qualities. This is an example of personification. I'm wondering why the poet chose to make the shoes and bed talk. That's curious and makes me want to read on. Also, it says the man was a good, God-fearing man and that makes me think he is honest and ethical—that he has good values. That makes me feel like he must be a good person in the way he thinks and the way he acts. Do you see how the language Ted Kooser used helped me to visualize and respond to the poem?" Most students nodded. "Okay let's read the next four lines and this time some of you will share how you interpreted images and responses." Ms. Snow read aloud:

says the Bible with a broken back
on the floor below the window, dusty with sun;
but not a man for farming, say the fields
cluttered with boulders and the leaky barn.

She selects some volunteers for a demonstration. "Kara, Dan, Raoul, Mara, bring your chairs up to the front of the room. You are going to help me model the strategy we are going to use with this poem. It's called **Save the Last Word for Me**. First, I'd like you all to select one line that interests you."

Raoul said, "I chose the line 'but not a man for farming, say the fields.'"

Ms. Snow stopped Raoul. "Don't say any more; don't tell us why you chose that line. Now Mara, you have up to one minute to react or respond to this line.

Mara thought for a moment. "Why would someone who's not good at farming live on a farm? Why did he become a farmer?"

Next, Dan weighed in. "It seems like they're poor."

After Kara wondered if the guy maybe inherited the farm, it was Raoul's turn again.

"So, Raoul, why did you select the line? You get the last word."

"The fields talk like they're telling on the guy. Like it's the evidence that he is a guy who isn't a good farmer, but the poet doesn't have to say it."

"Okay, good. So how does the poet use language to help you 'see' that image?"

Raoul answered, "I can see fields that have rocks in them instead of crops, and a barn that needs a new roof because it has leaks in it."

"Thank you. Now, in the next part of the class you are all going to use this strategy called **Save the Last Word for Me**. It is a two-part strategy—first you work by yourselves and then you will work with others in a group of four."

"Here's how Part 1 works. Select two lines from the rest of the poem that strike you as particularly powerful. Choose lines that generate a strong image for you. I am going to give each of you a copy of the poem and two index cards. On one side of each card you will write a line that strikes you. On the other, write what you think the line means and how the author uses language to create the image. Use the terms we discussed—*figurative language, symbols, imagery,* and *tone*—or you might use the terms *personification* or *metaphor*—some deep thinking about the imagery in two powerful lines that you select—for how Ted Kooser, the poet, uses language to make it happen. Note which stanza of the poem contains the lines you selected. You will be sharing your lines in small groups in a few minutes when we do Part 2 of **Save the Last Word for Me**." Students begin to select their lines and write the reasons for their choices.

After Reading/Learning

"Now I'd like you to form groups of four. One person will read one of their quotations and ask others to respond. When they finish, the person who read a quote gets the last word."

Students began working but there was some confusion about the process, so Ms. Snow stopped by several desks and prompted students to only read the quote, not the reason, before the group discussion. Slowly the group discussions began to flow smoothly as students discussed the poem and she noticed that several had selected the same lines.

As Ms. Snow circulated around the room she heard students' thinking out loud. "I think 'and the winter's cold, say the rags in the window frames.' The image that is created seems sad and lonely. And the way the rags are talking."

Ms. Snow notes that some of the groups are finished and some are still doing rounds of **Save the Last Word for Me**. "I am sorry to interrupt those of you who have not finished your rounds of discussion, but I need to give you directions on how to finish up our work before the end of class. The next step is to work together as a group to do a **Quick Write**. You need to identify a notetaker to record the group's thinking. Here are the directions for the Quick Write:

1. The group will choose four lines in the poem, one each that exemplifies the ways we spoke about the poet's work with language: figurative language, imagery, symbolism, and tone. The notetaker will record the line of the poem and the type of language convention associated with the selected line.

2. The notetaker will record the group consensus for the gist of each stanza (1–3) by completing this sentence starter: This stanza was about . . ."

As the period ended, Ms. Snow checked in to see how students liked the **Save the Last Word for Me** discussion and complimented the groups. "You have done some great 'meaning making' and interpretation in your groups. Your discussions of the quotations clearly showed you grasped the author's meaning. So what did you think of this strategy? How did it affect your engagement with the poem or your thinking about what it meant?"

When reflecting on the class, Ms. Snow thought the level of discussion and engagement for this poem boded well for the poetry unit, and she was glad she had tried the collaborative routine.

REFERENCES

ACT. (2006). *Reading between the lines: What the ACT reveals about college readiness in reading.* Retrieved from www.act.org/research/policymakers/reports/reading.html

Adler, M. J. (1982). *The Paideia proposal: An educational manifesto.* New York, NY: Touchstone.

Anders, P. L., & Bos, C. S. (1986). Semantic feature analysis: An interactive strategy for vocabulary development and text comprehension. *Journal of Reading, 29*(7), 610–616.

Aronson, E., Blaney, N., Stephin, C., Sikes, J., & Snapp, M. (1978). *The jigsaw classroom.* Beverly Hills, CA: Sage.

Baron, D., & Averette, P. (n.d.). *Save the last word for me.* Available at http://www.inacom-sby.net/def/PBE-Save-the-Last-Word-for-Me.aspx

Beck, I. L., McKeown, M. G., Hamilton, R. L., & Kucan, L. (1997). *Questioning the author: An approach for enhancing student engagement with text.* Newark, DE: International Reading Association.

Beck, I. L., McKeown, M. G., & Kucan, L. (2002). *Bringing words to life: Robust vocabulary instruction.* New York: Guilford Press.

Blachowicz, C.L.Z. (1986). Making connections: Alternatives to the vocabulary notebook. *Journal of Reading, 29*(7), 643–649.

Buehl, D. (2009). *Classroom strategies for interactive learning* (3rd ed.). Newark, DE: International Reading Association.

Burke, J. (2002). *Reader's handbook: A student guide for reading and learning.* Wilmington, MA: Great Source Education Group.

Carnegie Council on Advancing Adolescent Literacy. (2009). *Time to act: An agenda for advancing adolescent literacy for college and career success.* New York: Carnegie Corporation of New York.

Carr, E. G., & Ogle, D. (1987). KWL plus: A strategy for comprehension and summarization. *Journal of Reading, 30*(7), 626–631.

Clarke, J. H. (1991). Using visual organizers to focus on thinking. *Journal of Reading, 34*(7), 526–534.

Cochran, D., & Conklin, J. (2007). A new Bloom: Transforming learning. *Learning & Leading with Technology, 34*(5), 22–25.

Common Core State Standards. (2010). *English language arts & literacy in history/social studies, science, and technical subjects: Appendix A: Research supporting key elements of the standards; glossary of terms.* Retrieved from www.corestandards.org/assets/Appendix_A.pdf

Common Core State Standards Initiative. (2015a). *Development process*. Retrieved from www
.corestandards.org/about-the-standards/development-process/

Common Core State Standards Initiative. (2015b). *Frequently asked questions*. Retrieved from www
.corestandards.org/about-the-standards/frequently-asked-questions/

Common Core State Standards Initiative. (2015c). *Read the standards*. Retrieved from www
.corestandards.org/read-the-standards/

Council of Chief State School Officers. (2010). *Adolescent literacy toolkit*. Retrieved from http://programs
.ccsso.org/projects/adolescent_literacy_toolkit/

Duffelmeyer, F. A., & Baum, D. D. (1992). The extended anticipation guide revisited. *Journal of Reading,
35*(8), 654–656.

Duthie, J. (1986). The Web: A powerful tool for teaching and evaluation of the expository essay. *History
and Social Science Teacher, 21*(4), 232–236.

Fisher, D., Frey, N., & Lapp, D. (2009). Meeting AYP in a high-need school: A formative experiment. *Journal
of Adolescent & Adult Literacy, 52*(5), 386–396.

Frayer, D., Frederick, W. C., & Klausmeier, H. J. (1969). *A schema for testing the level of cognitive mastery*.
Madison: Wisconsin Center for Education Research.

Gillet, J. W., & Kita, M. J. (1979). Words, kids, and categories. *The Reading Teacher, 32*(5), 538–542.

Herber, H. L. (1978). *Teaching reading in the content areas* (2nd ed.). Englewood Cliffs, NJ: Prentice-Hall.

Hyerle, D. (1996). *Visual tools for constructing knowledge*. Alexandria, VA: Association for Supervision and
Curriculum Development.

Irvin, J. L., Meltzer, J., & Dukes, M. S. (2007). *Taking action on adolescent literacy: An implementation guide
for school leaders*. Alexandria, VA: Association for Supervision and Curriculum Development.

Irvin, J. L., Meltzer, J., Mickler, M. J., Phillips, M., & Dean, N. (2009). *Meeting the challenge of adolescent
literacy: Practical ideas for literacy leaders*. Newark, DE: International Reading Association.

Lyman, F. (1981). The responsive classroom discussion: The inclusion of all students. *Mainstreaming
Digest*. College Park: University of Maryland.

McEwan, E. (2001). *Raising reading achievement in middle and high schools*. Thousand Oaks, CA: Corwin
Press.

MetaMetrics. (2015). *The Lexile framework for reading*. Retrieved from www.lexile.com/

Palincsar, A. S., & Brown, A. L. (1984). Reciprocal teaching of comprehension-fostering and
comprehension-monitoring activities. *Cognition and Instruction, 1*(2), 117–175.

Partnership for Assessment of Readiness for College and Careers. (2012). *PARCC model content
frameworks: English language arts/literacy grades 3–11* (Version 2.0). Retrieved from http://
parcconline.org/resources/educator-resources/model-content-frameworks

Partnership for Assessment of Readiness for College and Careers. (2015). *ELA model content frameworks*.
Retrieved from www.parcconline.org/mcf/english-language-artsliteracy/structure-model-content-
frameworks-elaliteracy

Pauk, W. (1962). *How to study in college*. Boston, MA: Houghton Mifflin.

Raphael, T. E. (1982). Question-answering strategies for children. *The Reading Teacher, 36*(2), 186–190.

Raphael, T. E. (1984). Teaching learners about sources of information for answering comprehension questions. *Journal of Reading, 27*(4), 303–311.

Reading Quest. (2015). *Strategies for reading comprehension.* Retrieved from www.readingquest.org/strat/

Santa, C. M. (1988). *Content reading including study systems: Reading, writing and studying across the curriculum.* Dubuque, IA: Kendall/Hunt.

Vacca, R. T., & Vacca, J. L. (1993). *Content area reading* (4th ed.). New York, NY: HarperCollins.

ADDITIONAL RESOURCES

The following resources are some of our favorites to recommend to teachers of students in grades 4–12 who want to incorporate a strong focus on improving vocabulary development and reading comprehension into content teaching and learning.

Allen, J. (2007). *Inside words: Tools for teaching academic vocabulary, grades 4–12.* Portland, ME: Stenhouse.

Beers, K. (2003). *When kids can't read, what teachers can do: A guide for teachers 6–12.* Portsmouth, NH: Heinemann.

Beers, S., & Howell, L. (2003). *Reading strategies for the content areas.* Alexandria, VA: Association for Supervision and Curriculum Development.

Biancarosa, G., & Snow, C. E. (2004). *Reading next: A vision for action and research in middle and high school literacy* (2nd ed.). Washington, DC: Alliance for Excellent Education.

Bomer, R. (1995). *Time for meaning: Creating literate lives in middle and high school.* Portsmouth, NH: Heinemann.

Braselton, S., & Decker, B. C. (1994). Using graphic organizers to improve the reading of mathematics. *Reading Teacher, 48*(3), 276–281.

Buehl, D. (2009). *Classroom strategies for interactive learning* (3rd ed.). Newark, DE: International Reading Association.

Casner-Lotto, J., & Barrington, L. (2006). *Are they really ready to work? Employers' perspectives on the basic knowledge and applied skills of new entrants to the 21st century U.S. workforce.* Washington, DC: Partnership for 21st Century Skills.

Ciardiello, A. V. (2007). *Puzzle them first! Motivating adolescent readers with question-finding.* Newark, DE: International Reading Association.

Cochran, D., & Conklin, J. (2007). A new Bloom: Transforming learning. *Learning & Leading with Technology, 34*(5), 22–25.

Collins, V. L., Dickson, S. V., Simmons, D. C., & Kameenue, E. (2006). *Metacognition and its relation to reading comprehension: A synthesis of the research.* Eugene: University of Oregon.

Cotton, K. (1991). *Teaching thinking skills.* Retrieved from http://educationnorthwest.org/sites/default/files/TeachingThinkingSkills.pdf

Fielding, A., Schoenbach, R., & Jordan, M. (Eds.). (2003). *Building academic literacy: Lessons from reading apprenticeship classrooms, grades 6–12.* San Francisco, CA: Jossey-Bass.

Fisher, D., & Frey, N. (2008). *Better learning through structured teaching: A framework for the gradual release of responsibility.* Alexandria, VA: Association for Supervision and Curriculum Development.

Fisher, D., & Frey, N. (2008). *Improving adolescent literacy: Content area strategies at work* (2nd ed.). Upper Saddle River, NJ: Pearson.

Gallagher, K. (2003). *Reading reasons: Motivational mini-lessons for middle and high school.* Portland, ME: Stenhouse.

Harmon, J. M., Wood, K. D., & Hedrick, W. (2006). *Instructional strategies for teaching content vocabulary, grades 4–12.* Newark, DE: International Reading Association.

Harvey, S. (1998). *Nonfiction matters: Reading, writing, and research in grades 3–8.* Portland, ME: Stenhouse.

Harvey, S., & Goudvis, A. (2007). *Strategies that work: Teaching comprehension for understanding and engagement* (2nd ed.). Portland, ME: Stenhouse.

International Reading Association. (2006). *Standards for middle and high school literacy coaches.* Newark, DE: Author.

Irvin, J. L., Buehl, D. R., & Klemp, R. M. (2007). *Reading and the high school student: Strategies to enhance literacy* (2nd ed.). Boston, MA: Allyn and Bacon.

Irvin, J. L., Buehl, D. R., & Radcliffe, B. J. (2007). *Strategies to enhance literacy and learning in middle school content area classrooms* (3rd ed.). Boston, MA: Allyn and Bacon.

Irvin, J. L., Meltzer, J., & Dukes, M. (2007). *Taking action on adolescent literacy: An implementation guide for school leaders.* Alexandria, VA: Association for Supervision and Curriculum Development.

Irvin, J. L., Meltzer, J., Mickler, M. J., Phillips, M., & Dean, N. (2009). *Meeting the challenge of adolescent literacy: Practical ideas for literacy leaders.* Newark, DE: International Reading Association.

Jetton, T. L., & Dole, J. A. (Eds.). (2004). *Adolescent literacy research and practice.* New York, NY: The Guilford Press.

Kamil, M. L. (2003). *Adolescents and literacy: Reading for the 21st century.* Washington, DC: Alliance for Excellent Education.

Keene, E. O., & Zimmermann, S. (1997). *Mosaic of thought: Teaching comprehension in a reader's workshop.* Portsmouth, NH: Heinemann.

Lattimer, H. (2003). *Thinking through genre: Units of study in reading and writing workshops 4–12.* Portland, ME: Stenhouse.

Lent, R. C. (2009). *Literacy for real: Reading, thinking, and learning in the content areas.* New York, NY: Teachers College Press.

Marzano, R. J., & Pickering, D. J. (2005). *Building academic vocabulary: Teacher's manual.* Alexandria, VA: Association for Supervision and Curriculum Development.

Marzano, R. J., Pickering, D. J., & Pollock, J. E. (2001). *Classroom instruction that works: Research-based strategies for increasing student achievement.* Alexandria, VA: Association for Supervision and Curriculum Development.

Meltzer, J. (2001). *Supporting adolescent literacy across the content areas. Perspectives on policy and practice.* Providence, RI: The Education Alliance at Brown University.

Meltzer, J. (2002). *Adolescent literacy resources: Linking research and practice.* Providence, RI: The Education Alliance at Brown University.

Meltzer, J., & Hamann, E. T. (2005). *Meeting the literacy development needs of adolescent English language learners through content area learning part two: Focus on developing academic literacy habits and skills across the content areas.* Providence, RI: The Education Alliance at Brown University.

Meltzer, J., & Irvin, J. (2008). Supporting middle and high school teachers to provide quality content-literacy instruction. *The Exchange, 21*(1), 5–9.

Meltzer, J., & Phillips, M. (2008, September). Designing effective content-literacy professional development. *In Perspective.* Retrieved from www.ohiorc.org/adlit/InPerspective/Issue/2008–09/Article/feature.aspx

Meltzer, J., & Ziemba, S. (2006). Getting schoolwide literacy up and running. *Principal Leadership, 7*(1), 21–26.

Moore, D. W., Alvermann, D. E., & Hinchman, K. A. (2000). *Struggling adolescent readers: A collection of teaching strategies.* Newark, DE: International Reading Association.

Moore, D. W., Bean, T. W., Birdyshaw, D., & Rycik, J. A. (1999). *Adolescent literacy: A position statement for the Commission on Adolescent Literacy of the International Reading Association.* Newark, DE: International Reading Association.

National Reading Panel. (2000). *Teaching children to read: An evidence-based assessment of the scientific research literature on reading and its implications for reading instruction.* Washington, DC: National Reading Excellence Initiative.

Ogle, D., & Correa-Kovtun, A. (2010). Supporting English-language learners and struggling readers in content literacy with the "partner reading and content, too" routine. *The Reading Teacher, 63*(7), 532–542.

Pearson, P. D., & Gallagher, M. C. (1983). The instruction of reading comprehension. *Contemporary Educational Psychology, 8*(3), 317–344.

Phillips, M. (2003). Going for broke: 100% literacy. *Principal Leadership, 4*(3), 22–28.

Phillips, M. (2005). *Creating a culture of literacy: A guide for middle and high school principals.* Reston, VA: National Association of Secondary School Principals.

Phillips, M. (2006). Literacy: A key link to breakthrough status. *Principal Leadership, 6*(10), 36–40.

Plaut, S. (Ed.). (2009). *The right to literacy in secondary schools: Creating a culture of thinking.* New York, NY: Teachers College Press.

Public Consulting Group. (2015). *Paths to college and career.* Hoboken, NJ: John Wiley and Sons.

Robb, L. (2003). *Teaching reading in social studies, science, and math: Practical ways to weave comprehension strategies into your content area teaching.* New York, NY: Scholastic.

Roller, C. M. (1996). *Variability, not disability: Struggling readers in a workshop classroom.* Newark, DE: International Reading Association.

Smith, M. W., & Wilhelm, J. D. (2002). *"Reading don't fix no Chevys": Literacy in the lives of young men.* Portsmouth, NH: Heinemann.

Strong, R. W., Silver, H. F., Perini, M. J., & Tuculescu, G. M. (2002). *Reading for academic success: Powerful strategies for struggling, average, and advanced readers, grades 7–12.* Thousand Oaks, CA: Corwin Press.

Tierney, R. J., & Readence, J. E. (2000). *Reading strategies and practices: A compendium* (5th ed.). Needham Heights, MA: Allyn and Bacon.

Tovani, C. (2000). *I read it, but I don't get it: Comprehension strategies for adolescent readers.* Portland, ME: Stenhouse.

Tovani, C. (2004). *Do I really have to teach reading? Content comprehension, grades 6–12.* Portland, ME: Stenhouse.

Vacca, R. T., & Vacca, J. L. (1999). *Content area reading: Literacy and learning across the curriculum* (6th ed.). New York, NY: Longman.

Wiggins, G., & McTighe, J. (1998). *Understanding by design.* Alexandria, VA: Association for Supervision and Curriculum Development.

Wilhelm, J. D. (1997). *"You gotta BE the book": Teaching engaged and reflective reading with adolescents.* New York, NY: Teachers College Press.

Wood, K. D., & Harmon. J. M. (2001). *Strategies for integrating reading and writing in middle and high school classrooms.* Westerville, OH: National Middle School Association.

Wood, K. D., Lapp, D., Flood, J., & Taylor, D. B. (2008). *Guiding readers through text: Strategy guides for new times* (2nd ed.). Newark, DE: International Reading Association.